CAMBRIDGE LIBRARY COLLECTION

Books of enduring scholarly value

British and Irish History, Nineteenth Century

This series comprises contemporary or near-contemporary accounts of the political, economic and social history of the British Isles during the nineteenth century. It includes material on international diplomacy and trade, labour relations and the women's movement, developments in education and social welfare, religious emancipation, the justice system, and special events including the Great Exhibition of 1851.

Heathen England, and What To Do for It

This book, published in 1877, describes both the 'utterly Godless condition of the vast majority of the English nation' and the activities of William Booth (not yet famous as the founder of the Salvation Army, first named in 1878) at the Whitechapel Christian Mission, where he had been working since 1865. It is not clear whether Booth (1829–1912) actually wrote this book: the preface is signed by 'Geo. R.', and Booth is referred to in the third person, but it is conventionally ascribed to him and certainly echoes his own beliefs. (Booth's more famous 1890 work, In Darkest England and the Way Out (also reissued in this series) was ghostwritten by journalist W.T. Stead.) Using anecdotes from Whitechapel, the book claims that the British urban working classes are in more urgent need of Christian help and education, on the model provided by Booth, than any so-called pagan society overseas.

T0382298

Cambridge University Press has long been a pioneer in the reissuing of out-of-print titles from its own backlist, producing digital reprints of books that are still sought after by scholars and students but could not be reprinted economically using traditional technology. The Cambridge Library Collection extends this activity to a wider range of books which are still of importance to researchers and professionals, either for the source material they contain, or as landmarks in the history of their academic discipline.

Drawing from the world-renowned collections in the Cambridge University Library and other partner libraries, and guided by the advice of experts in each subject area, Cambridge University Press is using state-of-the-art scanning machines in its own Printing House to capture the content of each book selected for inclusion. The files are processed to give a consistently clear, crisp image, and the books finished to the high quality standard for which the Press is recognised around the world. The latest print-on-demand technology ensures that the books will remain available indefinitely, and that orders for single or multiple copies can quickly be supplied.

The Cambridge Library Collection brings back to life books of enduring scholarly value (including out-of-copyright works originally issued by other publishers) across a wide range of disciplines in the humanities and social sciences and in science and technology.

Heathen England, and What To Do for It

Being a Description of the Utterly Godless Condition
of the Vast Majority of the English Nation

WILLIAM BOOTH

CAMBRIDGE
UNIVERSITY PRESS

University Printing House, Cambridge, CB2 8BS, United Kingdom

Cambridge University Press is part of the University of Cambridge.

It furthers the University's mission by disseminating knowledge in the pursuit of
education, learning and research at the highest international levels of excellence.

www.cambridge.org
Information on this title: www.cambridge.org/9781108082327

© in this compilation Cambridge University Press 2018

This edition first published 1877
This digitally printed version 2018

ISBN 978-1-108-08232-7 Paperback

This book reproduces the text of the original edition. The content and language reflect
the beliefs, practices and terminology of their time, and have not been updated.

Cambridge University Press wishes to make clear that the book, unless originally published
by Cambridge, is not being republished by, in association or collaboration with,
or with the endorsement or approval of, the original publisher or its successors in title.

HEATHEN ENGLAND

AND WHAT TO DO FOR IT.

BEING A DESCRIPTION OF THE UTTERLY GODLESS CONDITION OF
THE VAST MAJORITY OF THE ENGLISH NATION, AND OF THE
ESTABLISHMENT, GROWTH, SYSTEM, AND SUCCESS OF
AN ORGANIZATION FOR ITS REGENERATION CON-
SISTING OF WORKING PEOPLE UNDER
THE SUPERINTENDENCE OF

WILLIAM BOOTH.

LONDON:

S. W. PARTRIDGE & CO., 9, PATERNOSTER ROW.

THE PEOPLE'S HALL, 272, WHITECHAPEL ROAD.

And may be ordered of any Bookseller.

1877.

HEATHEN ENGLAND.

In days when almost everything is disputed, when every-thing supernatural is repudiated as utterly absurd and impossible by so many, amongst the most educated as well as amongst the most ignorant, it behoves all who can pro-duce positive evidence of the existence and activity of miracle-working power to come forward, and to tell the truth and the whole truth.

I do not pretend to have seen paralytics, or blind men suddenly restored to the use of their physical faculties in the manner that pilgrims to Lourdes and other Popish shrines are said to have been. But I do place on record a story of cures far more complete and startling, wrought not in some far-off "corner," but in the presence of hundreds and thousands of spectators—amidst a blaze of gas-light, if not of daylight. For years I have been mixing daily with such scenes, and with people who have instantaneously received a power far exceeding all their bodily forces combined.

Most of this book was written a year ago, so that I have had ample opportunity to reconsider my assertions. What I say I know, and if, as I maintain, the statements of this book defy contradiction, they demand the immediate and closest attention, not merely of every man of science, but of every true patriot.

Read every word of it, and then, if you are inclined to dispute the truth of anything I have written, give me the opportunity to satisfy you, and to show you greater marvels still.

GEO. R.

272, *Whitechapel Road,*
London, E.

HEATHEN ENGLAND.

CHAPTER I.

WHAT THE PEOPLE THINK ABOUT RELIGION.

"Not for me!" said a strongly-built artizan one evening,
when asked to come to a religious service. And in these
three words he expressed as concisely as possible the attitude
of the millions in his state of life, with reference to God, and
godliness, and Heaven.

"But you know what we say is true, and you would not
like to be lost!"

"Oh, that's right enough"—then taking a glance at the
remainder of the crowd of men and women round about, he
bade us "good evening!"

Poor man! Living, working, walking, talking exclusively
almost with men and women who would as soon think of
flying as of going to a place of worship, and who watch
and ridicule, from morning to night, anybody else who
dares to do so.

It's all right enough. They ought to be religious; they
hope somehow they shall get to Heaven at last; but

nobody whom they know has anything to do with it, and they cannot face the whole world in arms against them and be separated from all their kinsfolk and acquaintance by this impassable gulf.

Those who mingle continually with people who regard it as almost an essential of their position in society to pay some regard to the Lord's Day and to the claims of religion, cannot easily realize the mountain difficulties that stand in the way of a working man's approach to God. The following description from his own lips of the inner conflict which a poor man endured before he found Christ may to some be the unveiling of a heathen life in their own land which they had little dreamt of :—

" When I first heard you people out in the open air you were singing—

'The gate is open wide for me,'

and I made fun of it, the same as many does. But after the singing I heard you speak and it went to my heart, and I thought, ' Shall I go inside 'with them ? ' But the Devil said ' No ; you mustn't be seen with *them !* '

" ' Well,' I said to myself, ' if they come and ask me, I think I will.'

"Then when you had done speaking, one of you came and asked me if I would come in, and I said ' No ; not to-night. I'll come some other time, perhaps ! '

" I stood for some time after you had gone, and there seemed to be two voices in me. One said, ' Go in,' and the other, ' No ; don't be such a fool ! '

" After awhile I thought, ' Well, I will go,' and I came to the hall door nearly. But then the Devil said, ' Don't go inside there,' and I stood on the pavement opposite till the man at the door said, ' Come along inside; ' and then I went in."

He was the only one of a large crowd which had listened to the Gospel with rapt attention outside who dared to follow the holy promptings which multitudes undoubtedly felt quite as powerfully as himself to leave the life of godlessness and start for Heaven that night.

The testimony of one after another of those with whom we meet who are Christ's is that " there is nobody in our works," " there is nobody in our house," " there is nobody in our family, that cares about religion but me." " They are all on top of me about it."

" Oh, sir ! " said a woman, when urged to give her heart to God, " what's the use of me trying ? I could not keep to it. I should go back and swear and curse to-morrow again, like all the other women where I work."

" But does not the death of one and another make some impression ? "

One Sunday morning I stood on the door step of a house where a poor woman lay dying. She had many a time ridiculed the speakers at the open-air services ; but now that the doctor had given her up, she was very anxious that some of these people should come and pray with her. As I stood there the newspaper boy came along with *Lloyd's,* and delivered one at this very house, for the lodger's Sunday entertainment while his landlady was passing into eternity !

It was no easy matter, while standing over the poor sinner's dying bed, making a last desperate effort to snatch her from ruin, to still the gossip of her neighbours, in the very chamber of death. They left the room and stood about the passage and the door till my visit was over, and then returned to gossip and drink with the poor creature till the end. This was not in some filthy court or alley. The house was as thoroughly respectable in position, construction and appearance, as any working man could wish. When the poor soul has fled they will tell you " she went off like a lamb ; " " she was quite resigned, poor dear ; " " she made a beautiful corpse," and so forth, and as they speak you will find the key to all this peace and repose and resignation in their own gin-reeking breath.

I turned from the door to a street not a minute's walk

away, where the Sunday market was in full course. Hundreds of just such women as I had come from, were making their purchases and chatting merrily, while a string of worshippers, marked out as distinctly by dress and appearance as by the direction they took, passed through to their churches and chapels.

Standing one Sunday morning in the middle of three streets of working men's houses, I saw a newspaper—often two or three—delivered at almost every door.

A good man, employed in some large guano works, was suddenly called home to his reward. Eight of his mates, out of respect for his character, bore his body to the grave, and decency required them also to accompany his widow to her mission hall for once. They came, primed to a man with intoxicating liquor, just sufficiently to make them impervious to any shaft of truth. They sat quietly until preaching was over, but the moment prayer began, rose and hurried away, lest they should be prevented from living as they had lived hitherto. Not one of them has been seen, to our knowledge, near any place of worship since, and they have one or two mates who would be only too glad to record the fact should it occur.

"I am sent for," wrote an Evangelist, in October, 1877, "late at night to go and see a poor woman who is dying. We make our way with some little difficulty through mud and slush into a dark corner on the very outskirts of the town ; but, dark and dirty as it was outside, it was worse inside. There lay a poor dear woman in the last stage of disease, with a family of seven children, and as I talked to her about her soul, I found that she was in complete ignorance of spiritual things. After praying with her she thanked me for my trouble, but wished me to be gone, as she could not bear talking to any more then, but would be glad to see me in the morning, when she hoped to be better able to attend to those things. The morning came, but before I got there her spirit had passed away."

Do they tell us of anything more dark and hopelessly heathenish than this in China or in Africa ?

There is a certain amount of infidelity spreading its deadly contagion amongst the unthinking. There is a considerable amount of prejudice against religion, arising in part from the inconsistency of its professors ; in part from a widely-spread notion that those who labour for the salvation of others are either " well paid for it," or are " gone mad with their religion." But the great obstacle to the progress of the work of God lies not in the incorrect views, but in the sinful hearts of the people. They " love darkness rather than light, because their deeds are evil ;" and when any of them are so far aroused from the sleep of sin as to desire to seek a better life, there comes in at once the dread of the rest to hedge them in. Amongst the working classes generally, it is an appalling fact that the separation between the people of Heaven and the people of Hell is already almost as complete as it will be when the Great Shepherd divides the sheep from the goats.

The continual sight of the half-ruined and perishing multitudes cannot but stir up every truly awakened soul to increased devotion every day. To stand in an open-air service and see a crowd of poor people, many a face clouded and twisted and marred by sin and sorrow, many a head turned aside to drop a tear as the word of God makes the poor heart quake, many a look of longing for salvation, or of despair as to its attainment—a solid mass of sinners, who know and feel bitterly enough that they *are* sinners, and listen for half-an-hour or an hour, as attentively as if they were in the walls of some sanctuary, to the preachers, and then to see all this crowd—to a man and to a woman— when the invitation is given to come inside, lingering, longing, wavering, listening with attention to the last sound of the procession as it marches singing away, or hastening off at the moment of conclusion, as if to escape arrest ; to a man and to a woman turning away to re-commence, as by a deliberate choice, once more the life which they know will end in everlasting death. Oh, that sight !—that awful sight ! It does not need that the fiends of Hell, that play so large a part in it, should visibly appear ; it does not need that any of that dying crowd should drop down before our eyes for that sight to be terrible enough to make anyone who believes in God, in Heaven, in Hell, determined to spend their latest breath, their last penny, their every available moment, in publishing the sinners' Friend.

But to live, and walk, and talk, and work amongst these people every day ; to know little children in petticoats who have learned to curse, swear, and fight—not street arabs—the children of well-paid artizans ; to see the little ones going to the public-house for father's beer, and, sipping it on the way home, so to acquire the taste for death to all that is good and true ; to know young men who are fast becoming drunkards and gamblers, and young women who laugh at the sound of shameless songs, and joke in language that would be shocking even from men ; to know men and women who constantly visit the public-house together or apart, who scarcely ever pass a Saturday and Sunday over without at least partial intoxication, who lavish money in tawdry fineries, and never have a pound in hand when out of work or sick ; to know old men and women, tottering on the brink of the grave, who pour forth their feeble indignation in the foulest language, who laugh and joke at the drunkenness and vice of their sons and daughters, and lodgers and neighbours, if they do not actively promote it, who have drink and tobacco brought to them down to their latest hour by dutiful children, as a tender tribute to their paternal worth and valuable training ; to know thousands of people who, though they may not be remarkable in any of these particulars, are joined to these people by the common fraternity of utter separation from everything connected with God, and by the common practice of ridiculing anyone who is not so separated ; to live and move all the day long amongst these children of Hell—is it not enough to make anybody who wishes to get to Heaven anxious to do anything and everything that can be done to snatch them from ruin ?

It is all one, whether you visit colliers, fishermen, mechanics, shopmen, warehousemen, soldiers, sailors, ironworkers, factory hands, brick-makers, navvies, or any other of the labouring classes. From one end of the country to another " there is no difference." The vast majority of your own fellow-countrymen take no notice whatever of the one God whose existence almost all admit. The " heathen " nations we hear of in other lands have, with scarcely an exception, Gods which are reverenced and worshipped. But thousands of your fellow-countrymen never voluntarily bowed their knee to any god in their lives. Am I not right in calling them heathen ? And what are you, if knowing all this, you do not do your utmost to turn them to the living and true God that made heaven and earth ?

Ah ! one thinks, if those who dwell in far different circles could but realize the havoc sin is making daily, hourly, amongst the masses, the splendid drawing-room and the comfortable club, and the busy counting-house—aye, and the cushioned pew, if not the lofty pulpit, would lose many a true lover of Jesus who would seek to follow Him, who, though He was rich, yet for our sakes became poor, that we, through His poverty, might become rich, and who has left us an example that we should walk in his steps.

OUR WAR SONG.

TUNE—*Men of Harlech.*

CHRISTIAN, rouse thee ! War is raging,
God and fiends are battle waging,
Every ransomed power engaging,
  Break the tempter's spell.

Dare ye still lie fondly dreaming,
Wrapt in ease and worldly scheming,
While the multitudes are streaming,
    Downwards into hell ?

Through the world resounding,
Let the Gospel sounding,
    Summon all,
    At Jesu's call.
His glorious cross surrounding,
Sons of God, earth's trifles leaving,
Be not faithless, but believing,
To your conquering Captain cleaving,
    Forward to the fight.

Lord, we come, and from Thee never,
Self nor earth our hearts shall sever ;
Thine entirely, Thine for ever,
    We will fight and die.
To a world of rebels dying,
Heaven, and hell, and God defying,
Everywhere we'll still be crying,
    " Will ye perish—why ?"

Hark ! I hear the warriors shouting,
Now the hosts of hell we're routing ;
Courage ! onward ! never doubting,
    We shall win the day.
See the foe before us falling,
Sinners on the Saviour calling,
Throwing off the bondage galling,
    Join our glad array.

CHAPTER II.

WHY THE PEOPLE DON'T "TURN RELIGIOUS."

How is it that whilst every religious denomination is increasing its buildings, its offerings, its Sunday Schools, its social meetings, its evangelistic efforts, there is such an utter and unmistakable separation between the church-going and the working-class population ?

In the first place, how few religious people really *care* about the matter. Just watch the dispersion of a large congregation some Sunday evening. Look at the well-dressed, comfortable, gladsome people. Observe their smiles as they say " Good evening " to one another. Their chatting is as merry as the whistling of the birds in the woods. They have had a good time—a charming discourse, a good attendance, exquisite singing, perhaps they have even had an " after-meeting " and seekers of salvation.

You see that row of young men who press through the throng ! A glance tells you *they* have had nothing to do with Jesus to-day. They are as well-dressed as the others ; but they do not mean to have religion, at any rate for a long time to come. Neither does that man with the meerschaum in his mouth, who pilots his wife and child through the knots of ex-worshippers. He prefers to take his wife out somewhere on a Sunday. The big rough men who follow

him, annoyed at the momentary obstruction of their pathway, express in oaths and curses their abhorrence of these
religious people and their sanctuary.

Now, does the minister, do any of the members, does
anyone, in fact, who has been in that place to-night feel
any discomfort because of the multitudes who have remained outside ? Is it not the simple solemn truth that the
matter never so much as occurs to the mind of any one
of them ?

" Well, but they *support* missions."

Just so, and with that they are satisfied. How much
does it cost each member of that Church to support the
missionary or Bible woman, whose pittance is small enough,
in all conscience, for the labour of visiting so many hours a
day ? And for this outlay the agent must not only undertake the performance of the duty, but also the responsibility
at·the Judgment-bar.

" But they have tract-districts."

Upon which they have the opportunity to assure themselves week by week that the people are still persisting in the
neglect of the means of grace, though politely receiving their
visits, tracts, and invitations.

" Well, how can they help it, if the people will not
come ? "

But does anyone put himself at all about to consider
whether it can be helped, or how ? You see that nice old
gentleman and his wife—dear, good people they are, too.
On their way home from evening service they will pass by
thousands of people who have spent the day in sinful
pleasure ; but the happy couple are busily engaged in dis-
cussing the evening's discourse and kindred themes, so that
the very fact of the sin and misery of the multitudes around
will never occur to their minds at all. And they represent,
fairly and properly, the vast majority of the most devoted of
church-going people.

But, then, suppose worshippers really did care to gather

into their churches the outside population (as it is now the
fashion to attempt for a week or two once a year) what
prospect would they have of success ?

To very many—on weekdays to almost all—working
people the very appearance of a place of worship, the dress
and comportment of its attendants, to say nothing of the
strange, quiet, regular, not to say stiff air which seems to
pervade the assembly, all these are circumstances calculated to produce a sense of discomfort and of absence
from home, not calculated to aid devotion, but to prevent a
second visit.

And then the service, beautifully fitted as it may be to en-
list the interest of those who have been accustomed to such
ministrations all their life ; admirably as it may be calculated to teach, and refresh and encourage minds already instructed on religious subjects, and which are on the outlook
for rational and heavenly food ; adjusted as it may be all
but perfectly to the taste of those who desire it, would in all
probability be quite out of the line of one who had had no
religious affinities hitherto. The music he might admire ;
but he would feel unable to join in its melodies ; the
prayers he might listen to ; but he could neither join in them
nor would they strike him as being aimed at his benefit ;
the sermon, supposing it to be understood, would be evidently intended to deal with persons in different circumstances altogether from his own, and the effect of the whole
put together, in spite of any amount of kindliness manifested
by doorkeepers, vergers, and the persons near whom he
might take a seat, would be to deepen the feeling that all
this kind of thing was for others, not for him.

Let those who have endeavoured by "special services,"
"missions," and so forth, to secure the attendance of strangers, ask themselves how many of those who never attend
places of worship were induced by extra effort to come even
to hear the extraordinary preachers announced ? And how
many of those who did come once, came a second time?

No, the working classes cannot be induced to attend ordinary religious services and ordinary places of worship, no matter how earnestly they may be invited to do so.   When the foundation stone of our Poplar Hall was laid, the Rev. W. Boyden, of the United Methodist Free Church, whose chapel was close by, " urged the claims of the Mission to the support of all Christians on the ground of its reaching a class of poor and neglected people not generally seen in places of worship."

Upon a similar occasion at Canning Town, the Rev. John Gostick (Wesleyan) " gave a loving address, speaking of the need of such a Mission, and remarked that it copied the example of Jesus by preaching the gospel to the poor.   He earnestly prayed God's blessing on the work of the Mission, and believed we should go on and prosper."

The same evening the Rev. T. Perfect, in whose chapel (Independent) the meeting was held, " expressed his pleasure to grant the loan of his chapel for such a purpose, and to take part in the meeting.   He believed God was on our side.   We must succeed because we went out into the highways and hedges and compelled men and women to hear of the love of Jesus."

From the *Croydon Chronicle* of 12th October, 1872, we cull the following remarks made at the Memorial Stone-laying.   The late Jno. Cobet, Esq. (Church of England), said : " Several Christian friends had long felt concerned for the spiritual destitution of the poor and working classes of Croydon who, as a body, are lamentably absent from our various churches and chapels, and as the existing means of grace had not reached them and were insufficient to do so, they suggested to Mr. Booth to take this work in hand. Notorious sinners who but for this aggressive missionary effort might never have been reached, have become converted unto God, and their present consistent life testifies to the reality of the change.   Drunkards have become sober ; thieves honest ; and blasphemers changed unto righteousness."

Nathaniel James Powell, Esq. (Congregationalist), who laid the stone, said : " He felt constrained to state that ever since he had known the Christian Mission, God's blessing seemed to have rested upon it, and His glory had been magnified by the work that had been done in connection therewith. He had been connected with the Mission for about seven years, and although he was not a preacher, he was sometimes called upon to assist in that good work, and he had always found his reward in that work. On looking around he saw many who had been blessed through the instrumentality of the Mission, and he could point out the great good they had effected in other places. Through its agency many persons were reached who were not accessible to other ministers of the gospel, and thus they were assisting others in the spread of religion."

At the evening meeting held in the Wesleyan Chapel (close to our site),

The Rev. J. Whiting (Congregationalist) gave a most energetic and stirring appeal on behalf of the claims of the Christian Mission to the support of all denominations of Evangelical Christians, on the strong ground of its reaching a class of our population seldom or never found in our more respectable places of worship.

The Rev. J. A. Spurgeon (Baptist) spoke of the warmth of spirit manifest in the Mission, as peculiarly agreeable to himself, and in tones of generous and cordial sympathy commended the objects of the Mission. He likened its missionaries, going out to the highways and hedges preaching the unsearchable riches of Christ, to the famous Uhlans of the German army ; as pioneers penetrating the very heart of the enemy's country, and preparing the way for the great army of God's ministers to come in and complete the work.

At the Annual Meeting, 1874, S. Morley, Esq. M.P., said : " I have long been connected, in a quiet way, with Mr. and Mrs. Booth, the originators of this Mission, and I have taken a deep interest in it, as it has helped, comforted, and probably strengthened many hundreds of persons depressed in condition and fighting for existence amidst great difficulties in the eastern portion of London. I believe in the sincerity of those connected with the Mission, and I am here this evening as a partner in the concern."

At the conclusion of the meeting, Mr. Morley, who was in the chair, added :—

" I do not profess to have much ability in reading countenances, but of this I am thoroughly satisfied, that many, if not nearly all here, have throughout this meeting, heartily rejoiced in the addresses delivered. The manifest earnestness and sincerity of those who have spoken, prove that they are men well adapted for the work, and I have heard enough to satisfy me that this Mission is (to an extent of which I had no idea) solving the question how to get at the people. As an Englishman, as a patriot, and as a Christian, I wish you every success in this good work, and pray that God may speed you yet more and more."

At the laying of the Stoke Newington Memorial Stone, the Rev. J. McKenny (Wesleyan Minister), whose Chapel is almost opposite our hall, said : " He believed the Mission preached the gospel fully and truly, and that our coming into the vicinity of the Wesleyan Chapel would be the means of stirring up the people to love and good works. He was sure that our coming would be a blessing to the neighbourhood, for drunkenness, crime, misery and iniquity would be lessened, and he trusted our utmost hopes would be realized in the salvation of many souls."

At the evening meeting, held in the Congregational Church, R. Paton, Esq., Presbyterian (late Hon. Sec. of the London Committee for Messrs. Moody & Sankey), said that, " while he did not see eye to eye with all the views and opinions of the Mission, yet he had found upon inspection, that a great and deep work was being done by it, and that he felt bound for that reason to give it his heartiest support. While all its sayings and doings might not exactly suit the taste of those who were accustomed to sit in such beautiful places of worship as they were now assembled in, it was manifestly adapted to the classes to whom it ministered, and for whom it was designed. And no matter how outrageous the operations might appear to outsiders, which attained the desired result, the Mission must keep on its course, and if one measure failed it must take up another, and so on, until the people were got at and saved.''

The Rev. J. Spensely (Congregationalist) said that, "instead of feeling that they conferred any honour upon the Mission by allowing them the use of the church on this occasion, it was the church which was honoured. The work which the Mission did, was such as many of them did not feel themselves at all qualified for, and such as they could not hope to succeed in ; but they would be exceeding glad if while they gave to the Mission their friendship and assistance, it could give them some hints which would be useful in enabling them to do more for the masses of the people themselves.''

Upon the occasion of the Hackney stone-laying, the Rev. W. Marshall (Congregationalist), whose church was lent us for the meeting, said :

" I do not feel able to speak, but I was anxious to come and say how very much sympathy I feel with the 'Mission. Though a Congregational minister, I am a Christian Mission man, and feel as heartily with you as though I were of no denomination, or of any other.

" The great question before the poor is, how to get bread. The knowledge they crave for, therefore, is of the lowest kind, and all their surroundings tend to keep them in ignorance. Hence the supreme importance and the arduous task of taking to them the highest knowledge, and teaching them what they ought to know of God and duty—such is the object of your Mission. The spirit of your Mission is the spirit of Divine philanthropy. It seeks to help the prisoner in the house of bondage, and to bind up the broken-hearted.

" Having such an opinion of your work, I rejoice to wish you God speed, and to tell you that I am one with you in the tenderest Christian fellowship.

" The Christian Church is dying of dignity.   All the life of Christ was the fullest and freest outflow of Divine love, and that chiefly to the publicans and sinners.   Such should be the life of his people now.   Let the Christians, rich and poor, of all denominations, get close together and close to Christ, and then, like a fire whose embers are put close together, the Christian community would become warm and powerful."

R. C. Morgan, Esq., editor of *The Christian,* after attending the annual meeting of 1875, wrote :

" We look back a dozen years, when Mr. Booth was called from his settled pastorate to this evangelistic enterprise, and we can but adore the glorious Power which has produced such great results, and gathered so many thousands of the poor into the Kingdom of God.   When he was asked where he would get his preachers from, he replied, ' Out of the public-house,' and so he has.   And when some of these rescued slaves of drink have been asked whence they expected to draw their congregations, they also have replied, ' Out of the public-house,' and so they have."

At the Hammersmith New Hall stone-laying, 1876, our tea-meeting was held in the lecture-room of a Baptist Church, and our public meeting in the Wesleyan Chapel.   At the latter, the Rev. W. Frith, of the Free Church of England, said :

" He was afraid the religious denominations, nowadays, were getting too ecclesiastical.   There were ' regions beyond,' masses beyond the pale of any ordinary religious influences. ' We fail to reach them.   They do not, will not come to hear us.   The only plan is to go out in the Apostolic way to get at them.   I am truly satisfied that your Mission reaches the crowds, and ought to have the sympathy of all God's people.   We have only to look around to-night to see how many men and women and young people your Mission has effectually dealt with here in Hammersmith. I am heartily glad to meet with so successful an agency. I thank God and take courage. I am convinced that you have got an agency the like of which is not to be found in all the regions around. If the facts connected with your work here were only made known to the wealthier Christians of this city, I should be ashamed of the name of a Christian if the Lord's people did not help their brethren heartily and liberally."

Terrible truth—the great Christian nation of the world is divided against itself, the vast majority of its people having no more connection with its religion, than they would if Druids ministered in St. Paul's, or Moslem mollahs hallooed from its church steeples ! A generation is rising up, educated as no former generation has been, in everything but religion, and trained by the immensely preponderating portion of their elders, to disregard religion altogether.

Is it not time for every Christian to awake to all this, and to consider whether anything can or cannot be done to alter so awful and so threatening a state of things ? Depend upon it, unless there is an alteration for the better, there will soon be a dreadful alteration for the worse.

The work of the Mission belongs to all, as it is for all ; and looking to the terrible need for the work which exists throughout the country, the all but universal lack of any successful effort of the kind, and the fearful consequences which must ensue, no matter how many churches, chapels and schools may be built and enlarged, if the masses of the people are allowed to grow up with this increasing distaste for all that pertains to God, we do not think it at all immodest or improper to say that we believe *The Christian* said rightly of us :—

"THE DOERS OF A WORK LIKE THIS DESERVE THE NATION'S AS WELL AS THE CHURCH'S THANKS, AND SHOULD FIND LIBERAL SUPPORT."

From the few examples thus given, it may be gathered that we have had the concurrent testimony of ministers and others of all religious denominations that their own organisations have failed to reach the classes we seek after, and that they have not, indeed, the qualifications needed for reaching them which the Mission has so fully exemplified.

Under such circumstances, was there any extravagance in the following language used in *The Christian* by its editor after attending our last annual meeting ?—

" A Mission of this extent, operating as it does upon the most neglected classes of society, turning scores of rough navvies and the like into preachers of Christ's gospel, and hundreds of the least cultivated and often most dangerous of the labouring population into respectable members of society and God-fearing men and women, is, as we have said on previous occasions, A NATIONAL SAFEGUARD WHICH OUGHT TO BE GENEROUSLY ENCOURAGED AND SUSTAINED. It is true these earnest men do their work in a rough way ; but men of culture would be powerless, with their delicate instruments, to touch the thick trees upon which these spiritual woodmen wield their axe with wonderful effect."

Will you read on, asking yourself whether these ministers and philanthropists are right in believing that the Christian Mission meets the great want ?   If you find the next chapter, an history dull, will you try another ?

CHAPTER III.

THE CHRISTIAN MISSION.

IT is scarcely possible for an organization to be devised beforehand to meet those peculiar circumstances which exist in society at various periods. God has contented himself with the general direction to his servants to go everywhere and gather all they can out of the world unto His kingdom, leaving it to them to adapt their measures and invitations to the various classes whom they may have to deal with.

And therefore we may notice how repeatedly individuals and societies, longing to accomplish some purpose of love for Him, have only by slow degrees, and patient, laboured efforts discovered the processes necessary and most calculated to ensure success. It is a matter for thankfulness that so much of past experience has been stored up for our benefit, and that entering into the labours of others for our Master we may hope at least to leave behind us a record which may aid the further progress of the great discovery which all the Lord's people must needs be so intent upon, and which even now seems so far from attainment—how to turn the tide of human thought and feeling to the largest possible extent in the direction of heaven.

The Christian Mission, although as yet but in its infancy, and having done but little throughout this crowded country

for the attainment of this great end, has, we think, become
sufficiently developed and established in the twelve years of
its past existence to demonstrate the value of certain appli-
ances for the salvation of souls. And if it should never, as
we trust under God it shall, mightily affect the whole population of the country by its own operations, yet at the least
it may serve as a torch to show Christians everywhere the
road into the ice-bound fastnesses where so many millions
of our own countrymen at present lie hid from the heat
and light of the Gospel.

The Mission originated, as nearly every useful movement
does, with one man, the Rev. W. Booth.

William Booth was born at Nottingham, in the year 1829.
He was brought up to attend the services of the Established
Church ; but at fourteen, with his father's consent, forsook
the Church for the Wesleyan Chapel, where about a year
later he was converted to God.

About this time, two or three youths, recently converted
had commenced meetings in the lower parts of the town, and
into this work, almost immediately after his conversion, he
threw himself with all his soul, preaching outside and in
all weathers. When seventeen he became an accredited
lay preacher. Two years later he was urged by the superintendent of the circuit to enter the ministry, but the
doctors thought him not strong enough, saying that if he
did so, twelve months would probably end his career. Under
these circumstances he resolved to wait, and in the meantime devoted himself as far as was possible to soul saving
work. For eighteen months he was wholly engaged preaching in London and in Lincolnshire, and at the age of twenty-
four entered the ministry of the Methodist New Connexion,
by whom he was stationed in London. But he had not been
there many weeks when the officials of the Guernsey Society,
having heard of his great success in winning souls, urgently
invited him to that island on a preaching excursion. He
commenced his labours on a Wednesday. Nothing remark-

able transpired for the first few days, beyond increasing congregations and deepening convictions; but on the Sabbath thirty persons professed salvation, and in a stay of ten days, it was estimated that no less than three hundred persons decided for God. The work spread like fire through the island, other denominations commenced special work, and a large ingathering of souls was the result.

The Guernsey people were most urgent for Mr. Booth's visit to be prolonged; but he was compelled to return to his circuit. The report of this wonderful movement, however, had spread in all directions, and led almost immediately afterwards to his visiting Longton, Hanley, Burslem, Newcastle-under-Lyme, Stoke, Oldbury, Bradford, Gateshead and Manchester for similar labour. So successful had Mr. Booth been in these places, and so evidently adapted for this kind of labour, that the Conference of the following year set him apart for the work of an evangelist, and in that capacity he visited Guernsey a second time, York, Sheffield, Dewsbury, Hunslet, Leeds, Halifax and Macclesfield. The ensuing Conference re-appointed him to the office, and Yarmouth, Sheffield, Birmingham, Nottingham, Chester, Bristol, Truro and Stafford were each for a time the scene of his labours.

The Methodist New Connexion Magazine and other prints of the year show that the following results attended his ministry. At Hanley " upwards of four hundred persons of all ages" were registered as converts. At Newcastle-under-Lyme, in "one week, 290." In Sheffield, during "four weeks, 663." At Halifax, "in four weeks, between four and five hundred." At Chester a congregation of a thousand was gathered every night, and "hundreds" sought salvation. Fifteen persons converted in connection with these labours are known to have entered the ministry of different denominations.

Some ministers, however, were opposed to the special services, which are now coming to be almost universally fashionable, and in deference to their wishes, Mr. Booth consented to return for a season to the regular pastoral work;

accordingly he spent a year in the Halifax second circuit, and three years at Gateshead-on-Tyne. At the latter place, a large congregation was established, and the society trebled during this time. But so deep were his convictions and those of his wife, that he could more effectually serve God and his generation as an evangelist, that he offered himself again for this work. And when the Conference of 1861 deliberately refused to allow him to return to that sphere, for which he had been proved so peculiarly adapted, and insisted upon his settling down permanently to the routine of a circuit, he resigned his position in the ministry, and went forth, trusting in God, to hold services wherever a door might open.

The next two years were mostly spent in Cornwall, where services, held in the chapels of various denominations, were blessed to the salvation of thousands of souls.

Whole neighbourhoods were stirred, religion became the all-absorbing topic of the hour, and the principal theme of conversation. Men left the mines and fields to seek mercy ; and in one case, a chapel had to be kept open from early morning till midnight for a week, so continuous was the rush of desperate seekers after God.

Mrs. Booth commenced preaching twelve months before Mr. Booth left the ministry, holding evangelistic services during that year in Durham, Newcastle-on-Tyne, East Hartlepool, and in Sunderland, in addition to regular preaching engagements at Gateshead.

During Mr. Booth's evangelistic tours, Mrs. Booth shared his labours; her ministry both then and since being marvellously popular, everywhere attracting crowded audiences, and leading large numbers to decision. How great a share she has had, publicly as well as privately, in the establishment of the Mission, will appear in the following pages.

From Cornwall Mr. and Mrs. Booth proceeded to Cardiff, Newport, Walsall, Birmingham, Leeds and various other places. Between two engagements Mr. Booth went to London in June 1865, and calling in at the office of *The Christian*, he was invited to hold a week's services in a tent erected in Whitechapel. Here he saw the enormous population of utterly godless people which swarmed on every side, and feeling his heart strangely drawn out for their salvation, he resolved in the strength of the Lord to turn aside from those who in all directions throughout the country would have invited him to continue the work of an evangelist in their midst, and to spend the remainder of his life in endeavouring to Christianize the millions of his countrymen who, instead of inviting, might be inclined to repel his labours.

We have seen how he had already gained considerable experience as to evangelistic work amongst various religious denominations; but he had little knowledge of the way to get at those who lay outside the sphere of existing religious organizations. All was to be learnt, with the careful hard-fought steps of actual engagement in the work. He had confidence in the Gospel of Christ, which is the power of God unto salvation to every one that believeth. That was enough.

He began by preaching in the open-air upon a piece of land by the side of the Mile End Road, where shows, shooting ranges, petty dealers, and quack doctors rival each other in attracting the attention of the poor. In those days it was rather a novelty for anyone to stand there statedly and regularly in all weathers to preach to the people. And this tall dark stranger who came to talk to them all familiarly about their souls, using every passing event and every common proverb to pass along the line of their ordinary thoughts, bringing in great truths long forgotten if ever known, was a new wonder—an attraction equal at any rate to punch-and-judy or the giant baby. Crowds surrounded him, and while he spoke, a Mightier far than he sent into the depths of many a dark soul the lightning flash of con-

viction. Men and women long burdened with sins followed
him to the tent, and one after another fell down at the feet
of Jesus and sought and found mercy. These, rallying
round their spiritual father in the open air, soon began by
their singing and their simple relation of God's pardoning
love to them, to increase the general interest in the affair,
and many who would have taken little notice of a mere
preacher stood speechless and astounded to hear men
who had been notorious for their iniquity, but a little
while before, tell of the peace and joy and love they now
possessed.

The autumn winds and rain soon demolished the tent ;
but the work went 'on in the open air. While a ring of
devoted men and women wrestled with God as they stood on
the ground, the power of the Holy Ghost repeatedly fell
upon those around, so that they were constrained to step
out before the staring crowd and then and there to submit
to God and seek His mercy.

Soon, however, an old dancing saloon was secured for in-
door services, and then a low public-house was purchased
entire and converted into a Mission Hall. These places were
small, but as people, crushed together on floors and stairs
and passages, listened with eager ears and hearts to catch
every sound, often from lips they could not see, the Spirit
smote great and small together, and many were daily added
to the Lord.

The time had come for a great advance, and God showed
a way. A large theatre hard by was taken for Sunday
afternoons and evenings, and there, by thousands, came old
and young, nearly all of them utterly unaccustomed to the
sound of the Gospel. Here, on the stage, by rows at a
time, poor sinners sought and found salvation.

As the fame of the work spread, hearers came, not merely
from the immediate neighbourhood, but from every part of
London, and especially from all its eastern districts. Saved
themselves, they naturally looked around amongst their

circle of daily associates and friends with longing hearts, and from Bethnal Green, and Limehouse, and Poplar, and Canning Town soon came pouring in earnest, undeniable entreaties for the commencement of similar work amongst the masses there.

The invariable answer was, " Well, see if you can get any room suitable for services, and let me know what it will cost, and I will come and see about it." To working people, who were determined to get something, this opened a pretty clear course. A club-room, a cellar, a shed, a back room behind a pigeon shop, an old abandoned chapel, an old factory, a schoolroom, a cottage, were just as eagerly sought after where nothing larger could be got, as the great theatre or music-hall. And in the most uncomfortable and most disreputable buildings, just as in the original and more desirable haunts of the Mission, the mighty power of God to save the vilest sinners was constantly exemplified in the most marvellous manner by the instrumentality of converted navvies and thieves, and infidels, and drunkards, and gipsies, and sailors, and butchers, and dog-fanciers—in short, the roughest, most ignorant, and wildest men and women who could well have been got together, and set up as witnesses for Him who had plucked them as brands from the burning. Twos and threes of such men soon were multiplied in each locality to strong bands of trained and indefatigable labourers.

In 1869, Mrs. Booth held services at Croydon, Hastings, and Brighton, and in each of these places Christians were stirred up to seek the salvation of souls with a diligence hitherto unknown to them. They asked for the establishment of a branch of the Mission in each case, and the request was complied with. After a few months, however, the evangelist and friends at Brighton thought proper to separate from the Mission, which ultimately resulted in the destruction of the work which had been accomplished.

Some of the Croydon converts, at the request of one of

their number who had removed to Bromley, rode over in a waggon to that place, and commenced services, which resulte d in the establishment of a branch of the Mission there.

Some of the Whitechapel converts removing to Old Ford, commenced a work there, which, after various successes, was at length brought to a close in 1874, by a dispute as to the ownership of the hall hired by us.

In 1870, services held by Mrs. Booth in Stoke Newington resulted in the commencement of a blessed work there, which has now for its head-quarters what was formerly a small brewery and public-house.

A gentleman from Tottenham, visiting the Shoreditch branch, and seeing the marvels wrought there, succeeded in securing the extension of the Mission to his own locality. But this outpost, where a brave, though never numerous band of workers was raised up, we never found it easy to use with a success commensurate to the labour involved in its maintenance, owing to the scattered character of the population, and we have, therefore, left the work entirely in the hands of the faithful few who will, we trust, be enabled still to continue in the open air and in-doors alike their constant testimony for the Master.

At Stratford and Millwall, spiritual work commenced by two gentlemen for the benefit of their workmen, was taken up by the Mission ; and although only very small buildings are available in each case, a very notable work has been done, and is likely to be carried on by the little companies of converts, who have been gathered from the world, and trained, amidst difficulty and opposition of the fiercest character, to stand their ground.

In 1870, the Mission acquired its largest portion of earthly goods—the People's Market at Whitechapel, a building fitted to accommodate 2,000 people, which has served well as the head-quarters of the movement.

From the Hastings branch grew, in 1871, a small one at Ninfield, a country village ten miles away, where the first hall built expressly for the mission was opened, the labour and materials having been largely supplied by the poor, simple-hearted servants of the Lord on the spot. Various other villages, and the town of Rye have also been missioned from this centre.

In 1872, halls were built or commenced at Croydon, Canning Town, and Poplar, which afford accommodation for some 1,200 people.

As a result of services held in Tunbridge Wells by Mrs. Booth, a work was commenced in The Lew, a low square of that town, where persistent daily preaching and visitation by a devoted young man resulted in the conversion of more than 100 of the poorest people, whom the Mission has, perhaps, ever dealt with as a body. Rag-pickers, clothes-peg makers, and all manner of tramps and riff-raff became devoted servants of God. The brother whose labours had been so blessed to them emigrated to Tasmania for the benefit of his health, and is now doing a good work there. But we were utterly unable, at the time of his departure, to supply his place, and, consequently, had to hand over the work to the care of a religious denomination.

Eighteen Hundred and Seventy-three will always be memorable in the history of the mission, for it witnessed an almost complete transformation in the aspect of the whole. The illness of Mr. Booth, in 1872, laying him aside for months entirely from the work, had very seriously affected the whole character of the movement. Several evangelists, recruited from various religious denominations, had come, bringing with all their piety and devotion an amount of inclination towards the settled, methodical, and unenterprising church life which they had left. The Mission was, therefore, being influenced towards the substitution of rule and system for life and energy, which must, sooner or later, have extinguished its usefulness to the multitude.

But, with the recovery of Mr. Booth, came the return of the old bias, away from the satisfaction and comforting of those already brought to Christ, to the training of them to further onslaughts upon the kingdom of darkness. 1873 was commenced with a stronger determination than ever to keep the Mission to its original aim—the spread of the Gospel amongst the masses.

Early in the year, Mrs. Booth began holding services in Portsmouth. For nearly four months she had gathered a congregation of some 3,000 people, in a low music-hall, frequented by soldiers and sailors and the worst of characters. From these services grew one of the largest and strongest branches of the Mission. In 1875, an attempt made by the evangelist in charge to establish himself as an independent pastor, and to divert from the Mission the halls hired for its services, produced a great deal of ill-feeling, and thus very seriously damaged the work. But, with the memory of Brighton before them, the executive of the Mission resolutely withstood this attempt, and the work in the town is now in a most vigorous and satisfactory condition.

Scarcely was the Portsmouth branch established, when Mrs. Booth commenced preaching at Chatham. Illness cut short her period of labour here ; but a branch of the Mission was again the result.

Happily, these two branches were organized by men who had been trained in the Mission itself, and who were, therefore, fully qualified to carry out and to enforce its orginal principles. The indirect effect of the work done by them was, therefore, of unspeakable value to the whole Mission, striking with death-blows the rising spirit of denominationalism, and arousing in the hearts of all the members a redoubled zeal for its great evangelistic purpose.

Meanwhile, a brother who had removed to Wellingboro', after trying, by open-air services, to do something for the people there, wrote entreating us to take up the work. At first, all we could do was to hold Sunday services ; but again the Lord raised up agents from the bosom of the Mission to carry on the work. At first, a young brother, with but slight experience, was the only one available for the post. He struggled nobly on, in spite of the most disheartening difficulties, his only place of meeting for some time being a tent put up on land which the rains reduced to a perfect quagmire. But at length an older man was set at liberty, and, under his faithful and diligent labours, the work was extended and consolidated.

In London, the spirit of holy aggression was breaking through the barriers of the past, and carrying the work into new localities with almost too rapid an overflow.

Now it was a little shop at Cubitt Town; then a charming chapel at Plaistow, abandoned by its pastor; next a wooden shed at North Woolwich, and at last, a little upper room at Barking, which attracted our attention, and into which mission preachers hurried, thinking only of the pressing need for securing the salvation of perishing souls.

The next year was a natural sequel to 1873. A great deal of hard toil to consolidate the fruits of the former year's vigorous advances; but, at the same time, further and even bolder steps to reach new neighbourhoods.

In Soho, where the whole population seems to be shrouded and overwhelmed in the dense fog-bank of drunkenness and sin, a little fortress was opened, where, perhaps the most valiant band of workers ever gathered in any branch of the Mission has toiled, with unflagging devotion and unquench-able zeal, to snatch brands from the burning, and, thank God, with no small success.

But the distinguishing mark of the year was the establish-ment of the Hammersmith work. Here a lady, who had long been aiming at the evangelization of the poor, had been per-suaded by her Bible-woman, a Mission convert, to invite us to assist by sending preachers for Sunday services. As soon as possible, however, an evangelist was placed there, and, in a year's time, some hundreds of sinners had yielded to the power of the Gospel, and a great body of working people were helping diligently to spread the glad tidings yet further

C

and further. From the first, too, this was done with very slight expenditure of the general funds of the Mission, friends in the neighbourhood supplying any little deficiency in the offerings of the people.

The work done at Wellingboro' had attracted attention in the neighbouring town of Kettering, and friends there who were desirous of missioning the town availed themselves of our assistance, and eventually agreed to support an evangelist.

The year had thus passed with comparatively little increase in the number of stations ; but the number of services held at each station had been increased very largely, and as the last days of the old year were fading into the first days of the new, a converted tinker at Stockton, a converted railway guard at Middlesbro', and a converted navvy at Cardiff were commencing what have since become large and powerful missions in each.

Eighteen Hundred and Seventy-five was made memorable by the development of these. In each town a large public building was taken for Sunday use, and, not only in the open air but in these places, thousands of those who had never before listened to the Gospel crowded to hear it, and, in the plainest and directest terms that one of their own class could use, heard God's condemnation of their sin and His offers of mercy. Hundreds of working people, converted in connection with these services, were organized into bands.

The sad events already referred to at Portsmouth, which darkened the record of 1875, and which were largely the cause of an illness which barred Mrs. Booth from active service during the greater part of the year, only proved, though by a painful test, how thoroughly the hearts of the great bulk of the mission people had become welded together, and how desirable and satisfactory to all were its foundations.

And the absence of Mr. Booth, an accident to whose knee confined him to the house for months, though naturally a very great drawback to the success of the year, showed forth by contrast with result of absence in 1872, the great progress which had been made in conforming the whole edifice so far to its original design.

A good hall was opened at Hackney this year.

In 1876 we took our stand in Leeds, Leicester, and Hartlepool. We did not, owing to various circumstances, gather so large congregations and so large a company of soldiers for the Lord from the public-houses and the streets as in Stockton and Middlesbro' the previous year, yet we trust the work, if a little slower in its early growth, will become perhaps even more solid and permanent in its character.

The only building of the year was a nice hall for week-night work at Hammersmith.

It was amongst the greatest joys of the year that Mrs. Booth, somewhat restored after long illness, was able to hold a series of services at Leicester, and that, when unable to preach any longer, her eldest son and daughter were able to step into her place and carry on the work.

. It was amongst its darkest shadows, however, that this effort, with a few subsequent services, overtaxed her strength, and removed her from the active list again for a time, soon, we trust, to be passed over ; and that Mr. Booth, borne to the borders of the grave by typhoid fever, was also for three months kept away from the field.

The enormous demand which the work makes upon body and mind and soul has always made it difficult to secure suitable agents, and has driven many who had for a season laboured with us to relinquish their posts. This want of a sufficiently numerous staff of evangelists is more and more felt, as the increased number of our stations renders it necessary for us to have a larger force than ever in order to keep up the efficiency of each place. Resignations, while not surprising to those who know the nature of the work, have been a cause of serious difficulty, rendering the further occupation of Kettering, Bromley and Rye impossible, and making it imperative for us to leave some other stations to be worked as best they may by friends on the spot.

But January, 1877, witnessed a novel resignation. Two evangelists had been entrusted with the work in Leicester. The elder one sent in his resignation by the hand of the younger, informing us at the same time that there was no longer any Christian Mission in the town of Leicester. His idea evidently was, that he could not only separate himself from the Mission, but, by taking the people who had been gathered together, form at once a local organization. It was too late, however, for this kind of thing to be practised again. An evangelist who had been placed at a small station for the year in the hope of restoring his health, enfeebled by rheumatic fever, when he heard of the miserable attempt, rose up and said—" No, we are in Leicester, and we will stop there. Send me, and if I have to lie on a table to preach, I will go. I'll sell the last coat off my back before the work there shall cease."

In a few days he was in the town with the young brother who, amidst the fiery ordeal, had stood by the Mission. Trusting in God, they laboured together, first in a little room that held only 200 people, and then in a large unused warehouse, estimated to hold 1,500, where hundreds have found salvation.

The progress of the Mission in 1877 has been more remarkable internally than externally. True, that the work begun in East Hartlepool in the previous year has not only been matured, but has led to the opening of a Mission in West Hartlepool. True, that the Stockton branch has been added to by the commencement of a station in South Stockton ; and that in Bradford and Whitby great congregations have been assembled, and a great and marvellous work done. But we really begin to look upon our extension into one town after another, and the aggregation in the course of twelve months labour, of a huge congregation of working

people and a powerful society on the spot as no longer a
wonder. We have found out how to do it now.

But what is most necessary, and what above all therefore
we delight in, is the growth· of that all-pervading, all-
consuming love to God and souls amongst our people, which
fits humble and uneducated men and women to go and seize
any town for their Lord. And the advance of the Mission
herein, during the year, cannot be expressed in any way. It
has found means of manifesting itself in locality after locality
by the beginning of noon-day open-air meetings on weekdays, in addition to all the services previously held, and by
the hundreds who have responded, again and again, to the
call to spend whole nights together in prayer.

Not the least significant event of the year was the death
and funeral of Miss Anderson ; the first evangelist who has
died in the work. She had only laboured at a station for a
few weeks, when inherent disease brought her faithful,
unflinching efforts to an end. She had been looked down
upon as a female preacher, even by some who ought to have
loved and valued her most. But when we buried her, a
large force of police was required to keep back the immense
concourse of people who, with every mark of respect and
reverence, surrounded her grave. A local paper estimated
that one-fourth of the adult population of the town gathered
on an ordinary work-day afternoon at the funeral of one who
was known as the true friend of the souls and bodies of the
poor. Oh, yes ! the people know the value of the faithful
ministry, even of a woman !

" But surely it is not all success and improvement ? "

Oh, no, still resignations. Two have come in to-day.
Difficulties by mountains, daily trials, losses of people, losses
of all sorts, even of stations now and then ; but we have lost
nothing of importance to the general efficiency of the work.
It may seriously be questioned whether the providence of
God, though in a manner undoubtedly " grievous," at the
moment, has not relieved us from the burden of efforts

begun in several districts with the best of motives, and prosecuted at no little sacrifice of strength and means, but which, for want of sufficiently numerous population or of large enough buildings for services, could never, humanly speaking, have attained large results. And there is no question at all that most of those who have gone out from us have done so because they had already ceased to be "of us."

But after all, the Mission has been a steady inroad upon the kingdom of the wicked one from the first to the present hour. Many a bitter lesson as well as many a sweet one has been learnt in the passage from the single open-air stand of July, 1865, to the large number of theatres, public halls, and other buildings, and to the hundreds of open-air positions occupied weekly now in town and country ; but the blessed sum total of all is that "the best of all is, God is with us," and we venture to say that He has shown in connection with our history how to do a spiritual work amongst the poor, such as had never been accomplished before. To His name be all the glory !

WHAT HAS BEEN DONE

FOR

HEATHEN ENGLAND

BY THE INSTRUMENTALITY OF

The Christian Mission

FROM ITS COMMENCEMENT

BY

ONE MAN,

On the 6th JULY, 1865, up to the end of 1877.

There have been established thirty missions, each holding hundreds of services in the open-air and in-doors annually ; the greater part of the expense connected with the hiring of buildings and the support of the evangelists, under whose leadership the work is carried on, being defrayed by those whom these missions directly benefit.

More than forty theatres, music halls, and other buildings have been brought into regular use for the purpose of religious services, thus providing comfortable accommodation for over twenty-five thousand of those who dislike ordinary places of worship.

Fifteen good, plain, substantial mission halls have been erected or purchased in neighbourhoods where no building suitable for our services could be rented. Towards the cost of each of these the poor have contributed their share in cash or in materials and labour.

Throughout every district of the East of

London, from Aldgate to Canning Town, and from the Thames to Stoke Newington, and in a number of large towns, including Chatham, Hastings, Portsmouth, Cardiff, Leicester, Leeds Bradford, Middlesbro', Stockton, and the Hartlepools, the Gospel of Christ has been proclaimed to the working classes in the streets, and in such buildings as have been obtainable.

Remembering that over 25,000 public services have been held during the past year alone, it would be difficult to form anything like an accurate estimate of the number of services held during the whole series of twelve years, or of the number of different persons thus reached with the Gospel.

It is certain, however, that the names and addresses of many thousands of persons have been recorded who have professed conversion at mission services, and that from amongst the ever-increasing ranks of these have come forth the large bands which now carry on the work, and who, from being drunkards, swearers, sabbath-breakers, and pleasure-seekers, have become upright, respectable members of society and earnest propagandists of true religion amongst their own class.

Nearly 700 of these habitually speak in public.

We have the names of no less than one hundred and five persons, most of them converted in connection with the services of the mission, who, after having been led by its instrumentality to devote their lives to the salvation of souls, have been **wholly employed in the work of God.** Of these, **thirty-one** are labouring as evangelists in connection with the mission itself, **sixty-six** ministers, missionaries, evangelists, Scripture readers, colporteurs, or Bible women in connection with various religious denominations and missions, and **eight** have completed their labours on earth and gone to reap their reward in heaven.

CHAPTER IV.

RELIGIOUS STREET FIGHTING.

" GET away, wid ye ! Get away, wid ye ! Can't a poor old
Irishwoman live in pace up this corner, without being
disturbed by you mission heretics ! You are everywhere !
The whole town is disturbed by you ! But away wid ye ;
you shall not stop here ! " (Nevertheless, they *did* stop.)

This old lady only expressed, in her vigorous way, the
feeling of many, many thousands who hear the Mission in
the open-air daily, a feeling which, ever and anon, finds
expression in a passing shout of " Go inside and stop there ! "
"You ought to be locked up ! " " It's disgraceful ! " " It's
all a mockery ! " " Take them away ! " Or at times more
mildly, through a policeman, who touches his hat and makes
a remark about " the inhabitants " (generally the *inhabitants*
of a neighbouring public-house), or through the smirking
lips of a man who, with a violent attempt at a solemn face,
intimates that " there's a man sick in that house " (sick of
the Gospel).

The Mission expects all this, and when it goes out marches
as to war " with the Cross of Jesus " (not a bit of gilded
wood) " going on before." The Mission would consider its
open-air services a miserable failure if they caused no
" obstruction " (especially to sin), or were *not* " a nuisance

to the inhabitants," especially to such of them as are made rich upon the misery and ruin of others. Therefore, the Mission goes to do open-air work fully expecting, though not seeking, opposition; and goes boldly, without forgetting, at the same time, the prudence which may be more useful perhaps than daring upon some occasions. "If you only knew," said a respectable sinner, " the terrors of hell that go through my soul when you sing past my house, you would surely give it up!"

In order to be the better prepared for resistance, the Mission generally adopts, when there are sufficient helpers present, formation in a ring, the leader of the meeting and speaker, for the time being, standing in the centre, those who compose the ring linking their arms should any appearance of active opposition arise.

But a determined leader, with only two or three helpers, can generally form and keep a good ring of the auditory, or can at least preserve a space in front of the speakers sufficiently large to let them be well seen and have room to walk about while they speak.

The meeting begins, as it is intended to continue, with a vigorous onslaught upon the sin and folly of the people, the opening hymn being such an one as :

> " We are bound for the land of the pure and the holy,
> The home of the happy, the kingdom of love ;
> Ye wanderers from God in the broad road of folly,
> Oh, say, will you go to the Eden above ? "

We are perfectly well aware that this style and tone of address is no more approved generally nowadays in the open-air than in-doors. It is the fashion to make use in the open-air even of such hymns, such topics, and such sounds as are deemed "loving," "inviting," "agreeable," "attractive," and so forth. Now, without going deeply into this matter, we simply ask anyone to observe the character of the congregations gathered in the open-air by the two methods,

We have not the shadow of a doubt that any thoughtful observer would agree with us that the working-class element is as remarkably absent from congregations attracted by the milder plan as it is preponderant where the more " objection-able" and " repulsive " system of truth is proclaimed.

How can people who have utterly separated themselves from religion for years, if ever they came in the slightest degree under its influence, be expected to find the description of the beautiful and sublime interesting ? But let them, after the manner of the Prophets, and Christ, and the Apostles, be at once charged in the plainest language avail-able with folly and sin, and their attention is sure to be secured, even when their enmity is also called forth. As a rule, however, to-day, as always, those appeals to the masses of the people are most likely to be listened to in breathless silence which most violently shake the conscience and prick the heart.

After prayer, *kneeling on the ground*, singing again. Everything short, sharp, striking, vigorous.

The speaking generally consists of a series of addresses, none of them exceeding five minutes in length, and with a verse or two of a hymn sung between each. Let the follow-ing, extracted from various copies of our magazines, be taken as representing such a meeting :

No. 1.—" You all know what I once was when I kept my shop open on Sundays—how I delighted in sin ; but now I am happy in Jesus, and if you want to know more about the change which has taken place, just come down to my place" giving name and address—" and ask my wife an' family."

No. 2.—" I was indeed low sunk in sin when the Lord saved me. Indeed, I was so miserable that I attempted to commit suicide ; but a man, seeing me by the canal side, called after me, ' Come away from there,' and compelled me to go home. Notwithstanding my sad state, however, when I was asked to attend the Mission services I said, ' I sha'n't go among those ranters ! ' But praise God, at length I was induced to go to an excursion, and I brought my flute with me. But I could not play that day; I felt wretched, and got no rest till I knelt down upon the grass and found salvation. Now, praise God! I stand opposite the very public house where I used to drink to preach, and when the publican would like to shift me, my old companions say, 'No; let him alone; we know he's right,· and he wants to do us good.'"

No. 3.—"Praise God! He can save farmers, too! The grace of God found me when I was hoeing turnips in a field. When I sought for mercy God said to me 'But you won't give up all?' 'Yes, I will,' I said; and the hunting, the silver spurs, the yellow kid gloves, and the silver-mounted whip were all put away. The last four months have been the happiest I ever had, and I am determined to do all I can for the glory of God and the salvation of souls."

No. 4.—"Well, I can tell you that God has saved a sailor, 53 years before the mast, a drunkard, and one of the worst men that ever lived. I have been in irons 90 days, have been in prisons in all parts of the world, and have had many a dozen lashes at the gangway in the service of the devil; but now God has saved my soul, and I'm on my way to glory."

No. 5.—"Thank God! He saved me when I was a potman standing behind the bar of a public-house! I was a drunkard, too, for I knew how to get into the cellar and have a 'skinful' of drink. I have been 'in college,' too— not in Oxford or Cambridge, but in gaol. And my soul was in prison, too; but now I am free, body and soul, I have got something to shout about. Many a time in the dark night I have crept about among the trees poaching; but now I love Jesus, and I can sing his praises."

No. 6.—"I don't think the men should have all the speaking to themselves. God has got my heart, and I am sure He shall keep it, for Jesus is the best friend in the world. My husband said to me, one day, 'I'm going to chapel, to give up all for Jesus.' He could not get me to go with him ; but his words set me thinking about my good old mother. I sat sewing when my boy brought home the news that his father had got converted. I got on my knees alone to pray, and then went to bed. When my husband came home he wanted me to get up and pray ; but I wanted to keep my soul's trouble all to myself. But I couldn't sleep. I lay there and wet my pillow with my tears. Ah ! those are the tears God wants to see shed ! In the morning I got on my knees, and sought and found salvation."

No. 7.—" Christ is *my* salvation. I am not hoping to be saved. I *am* saved by the Blood of the Lamb. My wife is on the way to heaven, too. My mother, when she was a-dying, clapped her hands and said, ' Praise His Holy Name.' That's the religion for me ! Seven of the family are on the way to heaven, too. When I was in the world I thought I knew more than most folks, but when I came to Jesus I found I was like a little wasp, knowing nothing and unable to do anything. Do you think, now, that religion unmans me ? Do I look any worse for being a Christian ? "

No. 8.—" God can save costermongers. I could scarcely read two words when the Lord saved my soul. The Spirit can change anyone as much as me. There must be a change of heart. If you only knew how happy the Lord makes us, you would at once give up your sins and come to Jesus."

No. 9.—" I think we are like a lot of rough trees in a wood that God has taken in hand, and he will make us beautiful by-and-bye. The devil led me far astray ; but I never forgot my dying mother's words, ' My boy, meet me in Heaven.' These words came into my mind once in the middle of a fight. The tears came into my eyes and I couldn't see to fight, and got beaten. Any time is God's time, and anyone can be saved. If God can save such a fellow as me, he can save anyone else."

No. 10.—" You perhaps think it a strange thing to see a black man stand up to speak for Jesus. It's pleasant to know that God gave His Son to suffer and die for us all, and that all are specified. There are multitudes of all nations in heaven. I have got a 'darkey' mother in heaven. She said when she was dying, 'Willie, meet me in heaven.' She prayed for me in death, and at last her prayers were answered. The devil was whipping me round this way—(running to the left)—but Jesus stopped me and turned me right round, and now I am running towards the Sun of Righteousness, which shines brightly on me."

No. 11.—" I heard the preaching in the open air, and was led to Christ, and there has been light ever since I came to Him. I have three little children gone to glory, and I am going to meet them there. My dear husband's gone there, too ! "

Need we say that we have not by any means reproduced the addresses as delivered, but have only brought out the distinctive features of such, omitting for brevity's sake also the earnest exhortation addressed by each to the people to give up the sins which were their curse, and to seek the Lord without delay.

But does all the speaking consist of relations of experience like this ?

By no means. That young woman has witnessed, a day or two ago, the sudden death of a workmate, the particulars of which she uses to impress upon all around the need for immediate preparation to meet God. That man has been reading to-day a striking passage of scripture or an interesting anecdote, which he uses with telling effect. A sister, with still greater mental power, reproduces to a huge spell-bound audience, one of our Lord's parables as if it were an affair of yesterday, and brings the tears from many eyes by her application of it. Another tells of some death-bed scenes she has just been witnessing.

Nor do the meetings always abound in these very brief speeches. Sometimes the bulk of those present are content to sing, leaving the speaking entirely to three or four, or even a smaller number of those who are qualified to take up the time usefully. We shall never, never forget seeing a stout thickset glass-worker step out one evening, and speak for half-an-hour or so upon the word " Eternity." As point after point was made clear and driven home upon the hearts of the people, many a poor sinner quailed beneath the truth, and when at last, dwelling upon the glorious future that awaited him, the old man seemed almost inclined to dance for joy, no one could but feel that when he was gone they would have lost a true friend, who had spoken to them in the power of God, and had taken a permanent place in their memory.

The evangelist or other person who leads the meeting is there to see that the truth as it is in Jesus, and that only is set forth, and set forth in such a way as to inform the darkest mind present of the two great facts which alone we profess to propound : that every man is a guilty hell-deserving sinner, and that there is a way of escape for him if he be willing to avail himself of it.

The frequent singing which is the rule with us, does much to create and sustain the interest of the meeting, and is necessary at the same time to express the unbounded joy of those who are taking part in the service. This unmistakable happiness, beaming from faces, which often bear as undeniable marks of former days of sin, has very often been found more impressive than anything that has been said or sung. "These people have got something that I haven't," is a constant reflection on the part of by-standers, and one which produces much fruit.

And the energy with which these lively hymns are sung and speeches delivered, while everyone in the ring continues in rapt attention throughout, convinces all that these happy people are in dead earnest too.

The speaking concluded, the indoor services are carefully announced, and then as a rule a procession is formed. The biggest men to the front, with one or two to keep troublesome lads away from the leader as he walks backwards conducting the singing, sisters in the centre, and a line or two of men at the back, or alternate lines of men and women—such is the general formation. Of course there are meetings and processions composed exclusively of sisters, or of brethren, and processions less remarkable for the numbers taking part in them, than for the unanimity and determination of those who do so.

" How many are considered necessary to undertake a procession ? " One. Jonah, some time ago, and stalwart evangelists of the Mission nowadays, demonstrate the powerful effect which processions of one can produce on a large town. The question is not one of quantity, but of quality. Half-a-dozen people linked arm-in-arm look anything but contemptible marching along an ordinary street. A dozen so arranged will cover its whole breadth and present the appearance of a larger company. Three or four persons walking silently in single file, as policemen do, may attract as much attention as a large band, and thus advertise their Saviour and their services as effectually. To procession singing is to be " a fool," therefore the only matter for consideration is the amount of good that can be done in spite of the prejudice which any procession of the kind is certain to create. Of course, for a large thoroughfare, a considerable number of persons is indispensable to make the procession seen or its singing heard above the din of traffic even on the Sabbath day. But such a procession as has swept along the Whitechapel Road nearly every Sunday evening for the last twelve years is in itself an instrumentality for good of incalculable power, and can never lose its interest and effect. It becomes, in fact, an " event " looked for and eagerly awaited by the people.

" But do not these processions cause roughs and lads to assemble ? Do they not lead to great opposition and disturbance, and embitter the minds of many against the work and the workers ? "

Unquestionably they do, and they are continually protested against upon these grounds. Lads, and even grown-up roughs, will sometimes form a large company in front or behind, and with hooting and whistling and singing of songs, almost, if not quite, drown the sound of the processional hymns. But what then ? A body of men and women cannot march through such a scene without arriving at their meeting stronger, happier, more confident, and more likely to be useful and persevering than if they had seen no war.

" Oh," said one, a couple of years since in one locality, " these processions must be stopped ; they only injure our work and keep people from coming near the place."

" That the processions must be well conducted—that all who can should take part in them in order to make them as impressive as possible, we admit," was the reply ; " but as to giving them up, if you will tell us how to make soldiers without marching, we will tell you how to make mission men without processions."

The brother who made these remarks has gone to a quieter place of worship. The processions he so disliked were only possible on Sundays then. A much larger company now sings down the same street to the same hall almost every night of the week.

Processions are indispensable to facilitate the passage of men who are convicted at the open-air service to the hall. They do not know the way, and upon this the Devil will base an insuperable argument against their coming, for they dare ask no one. Such people may almost invariably be noticed slinking along the pavement beside the procession, and once arrived at the hall door, they may rush in with the crowd ; or, at any rate, it only needs a glance this way and that to assure them that no one is looking, after all have passed in, and then for a plunge ! And this is saying nothing of the multitudes who, as a result of the procession alone, follow to the in-door service, or go home in bitter

D

anguish of soul on account of the sin which the sight of that triumphant host, or some snatch of their songs, has brought so vividly to mind.

Oh, yes; the thousands of processions which we now conduct annually, whatever care may be bestowed upon their improvement and the diminution of their drawbacks, these processions must be multiplied, as must also our prayers for those who would prefer "the peace of their neighbourhood" to the overturning of Satan's kingdom.

"How do you deal with opposition at your meetings?"

Generally by overpowering the opposer or opposers, as the case may be, by purely spiritual power.

We never reply to the objections of anyone, unless it be by bringing into our speaking in an indirect way an answer when likely to do good. Our general course is defined by one of our favourite choruses:

> "We have no other argument,
> We want no other plea:
> It is enough that Jesus died,
> And that he died for me."

An objection or question rarely comes from anyone but a drunkard or an infidel, to reply to either of whom would be a foolish waste of time. A drunkard will frequently be sent out to offer a glass or some remarks, but he rarely has sufficient steadfastness either of body or mind to persist when he finds that no notice whatever is taken of him. The sceptic will generally be hustled out of the crowd, if the people are interested, with the remark, "If you don't like it, why don't you go on?" When the bulk of the people are supernaturally held and dealt with, they will generally look after order even if the interrupter be not himself caught unawares and broken down before God. Many a drunkard and sceptic has come to our services in malice, and been filled with the love of God before the close of the day. "Being compelled to take a new route

one Sunday," wrote one of our evangelists, "for our
open-air work, to evade the police, we found ourselves
near the waterside among the roughest congregation I have
seen for many a day. Dirty men came out of the beershops;
unwashed children by the score crowded around us ; women
laughed and yelled ; costermongers howled out the price of
their wares. This, with our singing, made up the most
hideous noise I ever remember. Yet, in the midst of all,
tears were seen running down poor sinners' faces, which,
with the realization of the Master's presence, encouraged us
to go on. One man, a leader of a gang of labourers, was
so deeply affected that he went home, but for days could
scarcely eat or sleep. He sent for our people to go and pray
for him, and at last came himself to the meetings, where
he found deliverance. His wife is now with him on the road
to Heaven. He has succeeded at last in getting the roughest
to hear the Gospel. These are the sort of converts we
want !"

A young man who used to come out to the Fish-market
in Hastings with a newspaper, and pretend to read lessons
from it, and to hold a service, was laid hold of by the
Spirit of the Lord while engaged in his mockery, and was
soon after to be seen on his knees in the Market Hall crying
to God for mercy. He soon had the good news of pardoning
love to tell to everyone !

"But suppose the opposing force to be numerous, what
then ? "

We conquer by patient perseverance in well - doing.
Preacher-hunting is a grand diversion for any number of
weeks or months if the preachers make good running ; but
if they stand their ground doggedly and invincibly, it becomes uninteresting. To holloo and push for ten minutes
is delightful. If no impression be made, however, it
becomes rather trying in twenty minutes. In half-an-hour
it begins to be quite monotonous ; and, the moment anything else turns up (and something is always " turning up "

in a large town), the whole pack are off upon a new scent
(except those who are nailed to the spot in spite of themselves). This kind of thing may be repeated for a few
evenings; but, if the speakers and singers wield the sword
of the Spirit in Divine power, it will soon cease. A great
crowd of men and lads had assembled one evening for the
purpose of destroying an open-air meeting. Shouting and
pushing about were the means employed; but the preachers,
mostly women, stood their ground, and went on just as if
all were quiet.

"Had you not better go? This is no use," said a friendly
man.

"Oh, that will never do. It will be all right directly,"
was the reply. In half-an-hour the disturbers had all dis-
persed, leaving the immense crowd they had gathered us to
listen in the deepest silence.

"On Monday," recently reported one of our ex-navvy
evangelists, "just as we began to sing 'There is a fountain
filled with blood,' round came a brass band with some two
hundred following. We could scarcely hear ourselves speak
for the yells of drunken men and lads; but every time the
devil fetched breath we advertised the services, and so kept
our stand and stuck to the work." This at least can almost
always be done.

An open-air service was held one summer's afternoon
hard by a cricket-field, where some clowns were performing
at the wickets. A pouring shower drove both preachers
and cricketers under the shelter of a high wall; but the
preachers continued their service. Some who were thus
unwillingly brought into their congregation looked to the
clowns to relieve their distress by getting up a laugh. The
attempt was made; but when the speaker, turning full upon
the mockers, set forth in the might of God the great work
that had been done for him, and which could be done for
them too, the cricketers, with sudden desperation, made a
rush through the teeming rain for the nearest public-house!

Silent prayer has frequently been the means of stilling the tumult of the people. This was notably the case at Strood in 1874, when a band of rowdies who had threatened to throw the evangelist into the river, were suddenly hushed, as by an angel's breath, when their opponents knelt and silently besought God's blessing upon them.

But the victory which above all others we prize in the open air as well as elsewhere is the salvation of souls on the spot. We constantly invite seekers of salvation to come and kneel down in the midst of our ring before everybody, to plead for mercy. And thank God, the invitation has very often met with a hearty response! Our space will only allow us to insert one instance of this, which occurred in 1876.

At the Stockton races a visitor from Darlington was suddenly arrested by the unexpected strains of

> "Jesus, the name high over all,
> In hell, on earth, or sky,
> Angels and men before it fall,
> And devils fear and fly."

He had never joined in the singing of that hymn with all his heart. His father and mother had died happy in the Lord, and he himself had been a member of a Christian Church, but through bad company he had been a backslider for years, and had spent his time and money with the horse-racing fraternity. He had just put up his horse and trap at a public-house, and was on his way to the race-course when he heard that hymn. He said it came right to his heart. He trembled, and the tears rolled down the big man's face.

A prayer meeting was soon commenced in a brick-field by the roadside, and the man was invited into the ring. He came like a little child and knelt upon the clay, seeking Jesus. Many gazed with astonishment, and many wept while the poor man cried aloud for mercy. Soon his prayer was answered, and God restored to him the joys of His salvation. He went and harnessed his horse and returned home without seeing any of the races, but having beheld the Lamb of God, who taketh away the sin of the world.

What if the police come to put a stop to our open air work ? Our rule is instant obedience to any order the police may make, but examination and appeal afterwards if officers have exceeded their instructions, or if improper influences have led to their being sent out. When, however, it is found that the police are not merely instructed to remove us from any particular stand, but to prevent our standing at all in any neighbourhood it becomes a case of open war, and we have to accomplish our work as best we can. Of course, there are cases when quiet remonstrance, or refusal to move, may satisfactorily dispose of a fussy officer who has neither instructions nor reasons to justify his actions ; but, generally speaking, we find it easy to reconcile obedience with the perfect "execution of our duty." If we must not stand here, perhaps we may find as useful a spot not many yards away. If we must not stand anywhere, why then we must walk and preach as we walk, that is all.

At Hammersmith, where an arrangement of this kind has been very common, an open-air service had just commenced one Sunday morning, when a policeman stepped up, and after waiting in vain for a pause in the torrent of the speaker's eloquence, said—

"Now then, you know you're not allowed to stand here. Are you going to move ? The inhabitants complain very much." (Some of the shops just opposite were open.)

The speaker continued his address, while another member of the band stepped up to the officer, who after a word or two of conversation, walked over the way and looked on interested, though evidently disgusted at the hopeless failure of his authority.

"What did you say to him ? " the brother was asked after the service.

" Oh, I told him if he *would* move us, it would simply be a case of walking up and down."

No wonder the mere mention of this was enough for the poor policeman.

"*Up and down*" the little street, only 50 yards in length, and turning out of the main thoroughfare, the faithful band has paced, Sunday after Sunday, for months, walking as slowly as possible, dogged at every step by two policemen while singing and preaching by turns, just as if they were standing still before the large company who naturally assembled to see the strange sight. It is possible for the police to be compelled to do such work by "complaint of inhabitants," who do not hesitate to shock the eyes and ears of every decent passer by, with their brazen ungodliness. But it is impossible for policemen to enjoy such "duty." They would need to be as persistently kept moving as the poor missioners, to persist in such wretched and ridiculous performances, which only gain for us hearers and sympathy. And thus perhaps a few months of patient endurance and persistent conflict bring peace and quietness.

Not that mission men are not ready to be taken to the police station or police court when such seems likely to be the most useful plan. But, as a rule, serious trouble with the police arises from want of care and tact, and results in increased difficulties.

The interference of the authorities, after all, is often only the instrumentality God makes use of to stir up our nest, to rouse us up, and bear us on to some new locality. Missioners have a tendency to settle down to certain fixed open-air stands, just as other people have a tendency to settle down in certain pews. The stands may be excellent, unsurpassable, but to remain always at the same, is to leave many in contiguous streets entirely untouched. Anything, therefore, which breaks in upon the too rigidly established order of things, and compels people to "move on" elsewhere, is a mercy both to preachers and people, even if it be a mercy in disguise.

Indeed, no system of open-air services can completely arouse a whole neighbourhood which does not include constant and extensive "missioning," that is to say, going from street to street, and from court to court, speaking and singing a few minutes here and a few minutes there.

But missioning is rough work. At the finest open-air stands that can be used, multitudes may be gathered ; but multitudes who do not wish to hear may pass by. And the bulk of open-air congregations are generally *men*. The only way to reach the women—everybody, is to go to their very doors, and so to speak and sing that every word shall be distinctly heard in every room. To do this, however, is to find out as can be done in no other way, how many people detest the gospel, and how far their enmity will lead them to go.

An evangelist at Hammersmith, where the police have again and again attempted to prevent our standing still to preach at all, wrote thus—

"Recently we have made an attack on Ship Lane, one of the darkest streets in Hammersmith, where, from its appearance, the devil reigns supreme. Blasphemers curse, and drunkards stagger, while little shoeless children and haggard, wretched-looking women add to the misery of the scene. But one Sunday a band of us got down and woke up the lane with

'Jesus, the name high over all,
In hell, or earth, or sky.'

" Men, women and children rushed out to see what was up, and whilst one and another spoke of their precious souls, some wept on account of sin, and very soon after one offered us his cottage to hold a meeting, and, bless God, some gems have already been gathered from this neighbourhood. Two young women were induced to come to our hall, and they came boldly out for Christ, sought salvation, signed the temperance pledge, and went home happy. I was visiting the other evening, and a brother who lives there, said : 'Why you can't imagine the change there is down here since you came.' Pointing to a shop, he said, 'That man has shut his shop on Sundays, and a family that used to quarrel and fight have given over.' "

Another reports :

" ' Oh ! ' say the shop-keepers, 'there are those noisy people again. They are a perfect nuisance. We can neither serve our customers, make out our bills, nor do anything else. They were always bad enough, but since that woman has been here they are ten times worse than ever.'

" As we have no desire to stop any trade, save that which is dragging precious souls down to Hell, we leave these nervous shop-keepers, and march off singing to some of the back streets, where we again unfurl the blood-stained banner of the Cross ; but scarcely have we commenced, when a window above is opened, and a pail of water descends just at our feet, while our little band sing softly and sweetly—

> ' Living waters still are flowing
> Full and free for all mankind,
> Blessings sweet on all bestowing—
> All a welcome find.' "

At another station, while a brother knelt amongst the snow, praying, one evening, a shop-keeper came out, and, standing over him with a big stick, said, " If you don't leave off praying, I'll knock your brains out."

" Oh, you can't hurt me," replied the praying man ; " the Lord will take care of me," and continued to plead with God for the salvation of all around.

The shop-keeper now sent out a lad with a shovel, who heaped the snow and mud on the missioner, while a policeman stood by, remarking, " If you won't move when people wish you to do so, you must take the consequences," which, thank God, Mission people are most happy to do.

" But does any good come of this sort of thing ? "

Oh, yes ! We could multiply instances of the persons induced to come to the services, and eventually brought to Christ, by this missioning work in any one year. We prefer

to give an example of the numerous cases in 1876, in which
such work was blessed to those who cannot come out, and
would never, therefore, be reached so powerfully in any
other way.

"While going from street to street (at Milwall) preaching
in at window or door, or anywhere else, praying that it might
be a blessing to somebody, the Word reached a dear woman
lying on a bed of sickness. She was convinced of sin, and
so anxious to be saved that she sent for one of the brethren
to pray with her at one o'clock in the morning. She soon
got blessedly saved, and began preaching Christ to all who
came into the room."

Extremely cold, snowy, or wet weather, when it is impossible to get any large numbers to stand at a corner, and
when so many are in their warm dwellings, is a peculiarly
suitable time for this sort of work.

"But do you really recommend men and women to preach
in the open air in winter and in bad weather?"

Certainly, and why not? Our rule is, hold your service
unless and until you have found by trial that you cannot
get anyone to listen even at doors or windows, and that is
very seldom.

We should be amused, if we were not so horror-struck, to
hear grave announcements made, even by people who claim
to be authorities on the subject of open-air work that "*the
season is over.*" As though open-air work were a diversion
like grouse or partridge shooting!

The season over! What on earth does it mean? Look
at the crowds who fill the bar of every public-house, with the
cold draught from the great swinging doors continually let in
by some new comer! Look at the surging multitude pushing
about the pavement, and jamming the entrance of the music
hall and the theatre! Count the men and women sitting
in the covered yards of brewery taps, perfectly open to the
street, before the low tables that are just wide enough for
"refreshments" which destroy body and soul! Observe,

just as you pass by, the crowds gathered to laugh at the ribald songs and obscene jokes of the street comic or Christy Minstrel ! As you pass along, the butcher and cheese-monger of the poor, bustling up and down in front of their shops, will fill your ears with their cheery shouts, as line after line of women gather round them to " Buy, buy, buy," as they are continually exhorted to do. The lusty voice of the costermonger, male or female, who has been at it since the early morning and is not yet hoarse, will greet you in every side-street, and the comfortable " all-hot" of the chestnut and potato man surrounded by a waiting group, will make an impression on your memory. But, if your way home from such regions be ever so long, will you be able before you arrive there to imagine what people mean when they say " the open-air season is over "?

God forbid that we should discourage anyone from holding open-air services in June, because they hold none in December ; but God help the Christian Mission still to preach, and always to preach while the millions are streaming into hell !

There is rarely weather in which a crowd will not gather to listen to anybody who is anxious and able to speak to them, in the demonstration of the spirit and with power—and this our services, held regularly all the year round, continually prove.

The tremendous gale of November 14, 1875, which threw boiling waves over the lower part of Hastings, covering some of our open-air stands with water, and which was accompanied and followed by heavy showers of rain and snow, was reported to have "somewhat interfered with our open-air services. Nevertheless," the report went on, " the services have been fairly attended, and precious souls saved. After a very good open-air meeting at the East Hill, two young women came to the service held at Tanner's room, and, before leaving, they were enabled to accept the sinner's Friend as their Saviour."

" This is a cold spot ! " said a brother, one day in December, as we took our stand at the corner of two of the main thoroughfares of Chatham. And so it was, for the wind swept by in piercing blasts, no matter from which quarter it came. But there were the lines of Mission men and women standing in the mud, with the cold, piercing wind and sleet playing upon them with just as much effect as if they had all been ironclads. And in weather when one has heard people whine about not being "able to get the people to stand," navvies, and soldiers, and sailors crowded around as usual to hear those who were thus determined to be heard.

In the pouring rain, one Sunday evening, at Wellingborough, one of the Mission company, a sister, stood out in front of a crowd sheltering beneath an archway, and held them in the closest attention until it was time to proceed to the in-door meeting.

One bitter cold Sabbath morning in December, a Mission party entered in Bute Town, Cardiff, a locality similar to Ratcliff Highway, where hundreds of harlots and sailors live in open dissipation and sin. Soon doors were opened and windows lifted to listen to the message of mercy. In the evening service, an old man and his wife were noticed weeping. Asked to give their hearts to Jesus, they at once accepted the invitation and cast themselves at His feet. Their prayers were soon answered, light dawned, and Christ was accepted as a present Saviour. They afterwards said they were convinced when, unseen by the speaker, they were standing at their doors in the morning.

But let anyone who wishes to test the value of our winter open-air work come to any of our stations in London or the country any evening when such work seems likely to be "out of the question." Thank God, "He sendeth lightnings with the rain," spiritually as well as physically, whenever willing conductors are at His disposal.

We are sure it is unnecessary for us to point out that the men and women who do this kind of work are not of a particularly mild and gentle character. We trust they have learnt the meekness of forbearance and the gentleness of constant loving-kindness. But " they are a determined lot," as a by-stander recently remarked. They have been accustomed to run into sin with excess of riot, and they are now prepared for any lawful acts which may be deemed necessary to break down the kingdom of Satan and to establish the kingdom of Christ.

One of them, a great navvy, was met in the street one day by some acquaintances and knocked down over and over again to test his temper. A policeman suggested that he should give the men in charge. " Oh, no ; I'll leave them to the Lord," he said. But the same man expressed his state of feeling as to the work of God admirably when he called out at parting to a friend, " Hit the devil hard, mate ! "

A stalwart mission woman (whose husband is now undergoing penal servitude) might have been seen, after a journey of some four miles from home, standing in the mud, and speaking to a large crowd opposite an East-end public-house, one evening. She told the people how, a few years before, she had fought with a man just there, when drunk. No wonder that He who has done such great things for her finds in her now a willing servant for any service, however desperate it may be.

We are thankful to find that our people, not content with nightly service, are making a decided movement in the direction of establishing regular noonday meetings in various places. That in the neighbourhood of docks, factories, warehouses, workshops, multitudes of operatives can be brought together in the middle of the day with comparatively little labour, is so evident that our only wonder is that the idea of using such opportunities did not strike many of our evangelists long ago.

Great as have always been the signs and wonders witnessed in connection with the Whitechapel daily porch-meetings, we have never heard more startling stories than have reached us lately as to the results of such labours.

Again and again the patient husbandmen have been sent for to visit the dying in the hospital and home, who often " stood and trembled at the porch " without daring to enter in the presence of others to seek mercy. And still, day by day, there is the same rough crowd, the same eager, earnest looks, and the same scenes of turning away from and turning to the Lord.

But at the Triangle, Hackney, the crowds assembling time after time have, we think, surpassed in their variety of composition anything we can recollect. The well-dressed gentleman was there. Even young ladies ventured to linger for a moment on the outskirts of the strange crowd. Women who were evidently out shopping ; women who were bearing heavy burdens of work to or from the workshops ; women below the level of either shopping or work ; the farrier in his leathern apron ; the clever artizan ; the butcher ; the navvy ; the travelling tinker with his irons ; the waggoner watering his horses at the trough hard by, and lingering to hear all he could in a few minutes ; the rough ; the broken-down drunkard—all were there, and all listened with unbroken attention.

Such men and women, who have been saved from sin by means of such services, are ready to stand alone, if needs be, amongst a wondering crowd to publish Jesus. They reckon upon their open-air service every night, and are bitterly disappointed when unable to attend it, and God blesses, and ever will bless, such workers to the salvation of souls. " I wish there were more of them," said a superintendent of police once, when these " disturbers of the peace " were complained of. And so do we.

CHAPTER V.

RELIGION ON THE STAGE.

" WHAT ! preach in a theatre or a music-hall ! Hire a place from someone who makes a living largely from the sins of others, and then use it for God ! Can it be right ? "

Suppose the theatre, crammed full of people, were on fire —would it be right for a man to risk the destruction of his own body in an attempt to get some of the people out alive ? Does anyone doubt ?—surely not.

Well, here is a theatre full of people, the vast majority of whom are sinners in danger of burning in hell for ever. We cannot possibly provide another building of such capacity for them in the town, even supposing that we should be sure of securing their attendance there when opened to them. Then, is it not our bounden duty to gather them where alone we can get so large a number of them ?

When the converted railway guard, standing on the stage of the Middlesbro' Theatre, at his first appearance there, and asking who there could sing *truly*—

> " I do believe, I will believe,
> That Jesus died for me ;
> That on the Cross He shed His blood,
> From sin to set *me* free,"

saw only twenty-five hands go up from the huge assembly,

dare the very devil himself have asked, "What doest thou here ?"

It is surely time for those who love the name of Christ to ask themselves, Ought we really to bring every sinner we can to listen to the Gospel ? Will larger numbers come to hear it in a place of amusement than in a place of prayer? If so, ought we not to use these places at once, or to help others to use them by defraying expenses which the offerings of the people do not cover ? The moment this question is fairly examined by the Lord's people in the light of experience, one result only can follow.

" But how should a theatre be used ? "

The manager of a London one once said, " You should have a large choir to sing, for that is the way that congregations are got in London theatres."

But we have no such choirs. We should have a difficulty in mustering half a dozen people at any one of our stations, we fancy, who could read music from either old or new notation. Undoubtedly, we have multitudes of people who can sing together, with all the energy of soul and body, words which stir their hearts; but this is not the sort of singing which they call " attractive " in the religious world nowadays, so what must we do ?

We confess that we have not the slightest inclination, if we had the power, to place upon the stage of any theatre a mere human performance to draw the people and tickle their fancy. There are many places in London where, on a Sunday evening, those who wish for something interesting or entertaining, from a human point of view, may find it. But we have no desire ever to provide a " Sunday evening for the people " approaching, in the slightest degree, the performances of the Sunday League, or " Handel's Messiah."

We will not go on to the theatre stage, or anywhere else, with anything but Christ and Him crucified, and if that will not draw sufficiently, then we will rest content with whatever audiences we can get. We use the theatre simply to confront persons we could gather nowhere else with the very same truths we deal out in the open air and everywhere else, whether they will hear or whether they will forbear. And we find the power of the Holy Ghost still the huge, rough audience in theatre, or music-hall, or circus, and stir them to the innermost depths of their being under the preached word, just as if they were in some little parlour.

Indeed, what more suitable building could we possibly have, for close, thorough dealing with the heart ? Is not the whole construction of the place aimed at this very result. Every eye can see the preacher's face and every movement of his body. Every ear can catch his slightest whisper. The people seem all close around him, piled together like an open-air crowd. Even should there be far from a full house, the people present, if kept together in any part of the building, seem to be a complete audience close to him, instead of presenting the woe-begone desert, look of a hand-ful of folks in a large chapel or church. Now then, to a preacher who wants to see men pricked to the heart here is an opportunity indeed. Here are no doubt many needy sinners. They are close by. You can talk to them as though you were standing with each one alone, face to face. Everyone seems to be facing you, as if there were only the two of you present. Now, for life or for death, deal with that poor soul ! Tell him of his sin and danger till he quails before you. Tell him, then, of the Saviour's love for him, till you feel as though he cannot go away without giving God his heart. Plead with him as with your own brother. What stillness ! What solemnity ! Surely, there are but two. No, there are thousands ! And yet, every one of them is directly engaged with you, as though no one else were nigh. Oh, my God, save I beseech thee ! "Amen ! amen ! amen !" bursts forth from a hundred hearts at once. They have caught the magnetism of your feeling for that *one* you seem all along to be dealing with, and they feel as though all heaven and earth were awaiting the decision of one man there.

E

Now then, if you want to have that man and woman saved, you are as sure of them as if they were closeted with you alone ! They never dreamt of anything like this when they came into the theatre. They came to see what a theatre service was like, and now the Spirit of God has fallen upon their consciences, till they feel as though they neither dare stop nor go. A little personal persuasion, in the power of faith and prayer, and they will come anywhere, do anything, to find peace for their wretched souls.

What is to be done ? Hold an " after-meeting " of course. But what sort of an after-meeting ? A sort of quiet *conversazione ?* No, no ; you will lose that unspeakably valuable cohesion and priceless concentration of all round the speaker. Hold a simple, straightforward prayer-meeting, for the immediate salvation of every sinner present. Let as many of your praying people as it can accommodate kneel on the stage, and the remainder can soon gather in the front of the pit. Let every one who wants salvation be urged at once to come on to the stage, a passage to which from the pit should be formed in some way. The moment preaching is over, let an ample force of suitable persons be ready to watch every one who passes out of the doors, to hand them a little notice of the next service, and of the great truths that most concern them, but, more especially, to discover every convicted runaway, and pass him back on to the stage or, at any rate, into the pit. This same action can go on in every part of the house, between one and another. When those who stay to the prayer-meeting are settled in the pit, which generally suffices to contain them, and where they can generally be congregated, with a little management, during the singing of a hymn, a few words of urgent invitation to undecided sinners and believers may be useful before the prayer-meeting is regularly commenced. Then let everybody go down before God. No looking about, much less conversation, permitted, except on the part of those whose business it is to gather any sinners from the pit on to the stage, or to direct them there to Christ

Let there, in short, be just such a prayer-meeting, just such a penitent form, and just such action in every way as you would desire in a little mission room. The same faith in God will bring the same spiritual power, and the glorious scenes the Mission has, by God's help, placed on many a stage, can be reproduced with new actors every Sunday evening everywhere.

"But would not an inquiry-room be better than the stage?"

Certainly not. Any inquiry room is an admirable place for inquirers, for people who simply want to ask questions and get information; but when a sinner wants "a place for repentance," it is another thing altogether. His first necessity is to come out from his surroundings—practically, boldly, and as publicly as possible, to declare that he has done with them all, and means to begin a new life. The Devil will be delighted to persuade him he can do it all at home, or in some quiet corner, unseen. This is merely a clever contrivance to postpone the real battle, the separation from and renunciation of the world, the flesh and the devil, which must come before there can be any reconciliation with God. Give a man the opportunity by one bold step to finish the conflict raging in his breast, and at the same time to submit himself like a child to his God, then he wants a place to pray. It is not your talk to him, or his to you, that is to do the main part of the work. It is his intercourse with God that must determine whether he goes away pardoned or not.

Let only people who know how to help a poor seeking soul to reason with God, so as to get the scarlet stains washed away *now*, speak to anxious ones, and let all be as perfectly under the direction of one mind and will as in the preaching service. Then all may be conducted with as perfect decorum and success as you can desire in a mission room.

We have presented, as nearly as words can describe it, a mission theatre service. It only remains for us to record some of the scenes of our experience.

Says one who heard Mr. Booth in the Effingham Theatre, now the East London :

"Precisely at seven, Mr. Booth made his appearance in front of the foot-lights, and gave out the well-known hymn commencing, 'There is a better world, they say,' which was sung with an intensity and vigour which would have somewhat startled those accustomed only to the slow-measured Gregorian chants or dreamy tunes now so fashionable in most places of worship. Everybody seemed to join in the singing. They gloried in it, as if in so doing they for the moment forgot all the sorrows, cares, and woes of their daily life. Certainly, it was a strange sight : this vast multitude of hard-featured men and women in humble attire, in their working coats and in their tattered shawls, standing up amid all the dingy, tawdry tinselled surroundings, to sing of the better world where 'music fills the balmy air,' and 'angels with bright wings,' and 'harps of gold,' and 'mansions fair,' hold out the rich and glorious promise of future happiness. As the hymn proceeded, the strain became more and more earnest, until the lines—

> 'We may be cleansed from every sin,
> We may be crowned with bliss again,
> And in that land of pleasure reign,'

were reached, when it became almost pathetic in the emphasis bestowed upon it. The singers evidently felt what they sang, and as they reluctantly resumed their seats, a happier expression seemed to light up the broad sea of pale and careworn features which were turned with ardent, longing gaze towards the preacher and his colleagues. A short prayer followed, after which another hymn, 'The voice of Wisdom cries, Be in time,' was sung ; and then came the usual chapter from the Bible. Mr. Booth employed very simple language in his comments upon each verse read by him, and frequently repeated the same sentence several times, as if he was afraid his hearers would forget it. He told them that the devil was continually angling for man's soul—that he offered us wealth, pleasure, food, and every possible happiness upon earth, if we would but serve him; while God, on the contrary, promised us eternal happiness hereafter.

" It was curious to note the intense, almost painful, degree of eagerness with which every utterance of the speaker was listened to. The crowd seemed fearful of losing even a word. Another hymn, sung with redoubled fervour, and then the sermon commenced. In an impassioned discourse, the preacher bade his hearers come forth from among the wicked and be saved. He spoke of God's mercy and man's ingratitude, and declared that God was compelled to be unmerciful to the wicked unless they repented; that He could not help it if they refused to listen to Him. He told his hearers of their faults, of their vices, and threatened them with all the terrors of eternal punishment unless they repented them of their sins. He spoke of the happiness experienced by the converted, and described how in all our troubles, in all our cares, Jesus was an ever-ready Friend, affording peace and consolation to all who believed in Him. He also told them of a poor man, a pauper, dying in a cold and desolate room, with no one near him to moisten his dry, parched lips, or to bathe his clammy brow. Yet, although abandoned by man, he was not deserted by God. Angels hovered around his deathbed, irradiating it with their glory, and bore his soul, as it emerged from its senseless cell of clay, to the bright and glorious shores of heaven. And when the poor man again opened his eyes, and beheld the grand and beautiful mansions, the crowds of saints clad in their robes of white, and with their harps of gold, and heard the eternal song of rejoicing ascending to the great white throne of God the Father, he could scarcely believe himself. He, the poor outcast, who had dared to rely on the mercy of his Redeemer, actually in Heaven! Impossible! But it was true. And how. light seemed all his earthly trials, how paltry became all his earthly cares, how slight the weight of his cross, when his reward was a crown of happiness like to this!

" As the speaker described the picture of the poor man in heaven, breathless silence pervaded the ranks of his hearers. You might see great brawny-limbed roughs endeavouring, but in vain, to look unconcerned ; while, behind them, thin, gaunt-featured mechanics, made of less stubborn material, scarcely attempted to restrain the tears which glistened in their sunken eyes. Everybody seemed more or less affected. Here and there women were sobbing loudly, while others were looking with a strange rapt gaze at the speaker. It was a wonderful influence,—that possessed by the preacher over his hearers. Very unconventional in style, no doubt, it enabled him to reach the hearts of hundreds of those for whom the prison and the convicts' settlement have no terrors, of whom even the police stand in fear. It is a rough-and-ready style of preaching, but then the preacher has to do with rough-and-ready minds, upon which the subtleties of a refined discourse would be lost. If any proof of the effectiveness of Mr. Booth's preaching were required, it was afforded by the earnestness with which his hearers listened to the moral deduced by him from his text, in which he implored them, first, to leave their sins ; second, to leave them at once, that night ; and third, to come to Christ. Not a word that was uttered by him could be misunderstood ; not a doctrine was propounded which was beyond the comprehension of those to whom it was addressed. We might dispute the speaker's taste in some matters, we might differ from some of his theological views ; but his hearers were in nowise disposed to be critical. They listened to him with an amount of respect, attention, even eagerness, which conclusively demonstrated his mastery over their natures, his knowledge of their feelings, and the truth of his interpretation of their aspirations. There was no sign of impatience during the sermon. There was too much dramatic action, too much anecdotal matter, to admit of its being considered ' dull ' ; and when it terminated, scarcely a person left his seat. Indeed, some appeared to consider it too short, although the discourse had occupied fully an hour in its delivery ! The hymn which followed—

> ' Just as I am, without one plea,
> But that Thy blood was shed for me,
> And that Thou bid'st me come to Thee,
> . O Lamb of God, I come ! '

was sung with much feeling. Harmony there was little— noise there was plenty of ; but, after all, why should we cavil at these trifles ? Everybody wanted to sing, whether they possessed tuneful voices or not, and, where the *will* exists, let us not too sharply criticise the *way* in which it is developed. No sooner was the hymn over, than the nume- rous helpers whom Mr. Booth has gathered round him, and who belong almost exclusively to the poorer classes, began personally visiting all present, affectionately entreating them to join the band of believers in Christ's mercy. Nor were their efforts unsuccessful. Not a few went on to the stage and knelt in silent prayer. This continued for more than an hour, during which various prayers were offered up and several hymns sung. The dispersal of the audience was effected very slowly, and even so late as ten o'clock there were between two and three hundred people in the building ; but from first to last there was not the least interruption— not the shadow of an attempt at disorder. Surely this is something to be thankful for ; the olive-branch which tells us that ground has been discovered at last, and that there is hope in the future for those engaged in the good and praise- worthy work of evangelizing East London."

" I shall never forget," says another, who came over from the West-end for the occasion, "hearing Mr. Booth the first time he preached in the Effingham Theatre, Whitechapel.

" There were two open-air meetings in the Mile End

Road, and a procession to the theatre. It was a grand sight
when we got inside to look at the house crowded from ceiling
to floor. I had never seen Mr. Booth before that night,
though I had often heard of him. He commenced by giving
out the hymn—

> ' We are bound for the land
> Of the pure and the holy.'

"In the middle of the first verse he cried out to one of
his helpers, ' Flawn, shut that door !' He stopped giving
out another to say, ' Flawn, put those two young men out !'
In the course of another he came to a dead stop, and looked
up into a side gallery, combing his hair with his fingers.
All eyes were turned in the direction of some men who had
been misbehaving themselves, but who were thus put to
silence.

"By this time, the preacher had completely captured me,
and, I presume, nearly all the rest, although many of the
roughest East-enders were there out of pure curiosity to see
how he would do. We found we were not listening to 'a
parson,' who had so many hymns to give out, so many words
to say, and then done. It was *a man*, profoundly religious,
thoroughly in earnest, but able to talk to us about religion
without any sort of stiffness or formality, right from his
heart, and a man who was determined to be listened to and
to succeed.

"The singing was lively and powerful. Everybody seemed
to join in, which made it grand both in time and tune.

"The sermon was clear, pointed, definite and short, full of
life and power, thoroughly arousing, and very simple, being
mixed with touching anecdotes ; and it had its effect upon
the people. Many were awakened, and numbers saved."

"In October, 1867," says a third, "I heard that William
Booth was going to preach in the Pavilion Theatre on 'The
Blind Beggar.' My mother had often told me when I was a
lad, about the blind beggar of Bethnal Green, who was quite

blind, but whose daughter was so beautiful that a king married her. Thinks I, I would like to hear that tale again, I'll go and hear him. But lo and behold, when I got there, it was *me* that was the blind beggar.

" I can't remember anything of the sermon, except that he told about a young lady that leaned over a bank where there was a lot of water beneath, to pluck a flower, and lost her balance, and fell into the water. He said that was what drunkards and wife-beaters was a doing, and, thinks I, ' it's me he means.'

" In the prayer meeting he come to me and says :

" ' Well my friend, how are you ? '

" ' Oh, very well,' I says.

" ' But how is your soul ? '

" ' Oh, I don't know about that,' I says, and with that I came away. But I couldn't make it out him asking me how my soul was. Thinks I, I'll never go near him no more.

" I kept all on thinking about it all the way home, and when I got there my wife says to me, ' What, have you come home, and sober too ? '

" ' Yes,' says I, ' and it would have made you sober, or anybody else, to hear such a character as a man's been giving me.'

" I kept thinking about it all the next day, and I couldn't help going at night to hear him again in a hall they had up the Whitechapel Road. He seemed to be on to me worse than ever then, and I saw a man sitting on the platform that knew me. Ah, thinks I, That man's telling him every word of it. I'll let him have it when I see him in the docks to-morrow.'

" I came two or three more nights that week, and the next Sunday I went to the theatre again. I cannot remember anything about that service ; but I went on to the stage with forty-two more that night to seek mercy. They took down all our names and addresses."

The effect of the services, as thus described by one of the

darkest and hardest hearers who attended them, fairly represents the way in which theatre services of the Mission stamp strike the masses, who are aimed at, generally.

In the winter of 1873 a large circus was put up in the centre of the town of Hastings, and we hastened to take advantage of the opportunity thus afforded us of reaching the multitude.

Mrs. Booth occupied the platform on the first Sunday evening. She was just then in a very delicate state of health, "resting" at the seaside ; but no consideration could deter her from the enterprise when the open door presented itself.

Now, Hastings is scarcely the sort of town in which one would naturally expect to find a mission like ours. The labouring population is by no means so large or so rough as for our purposes we could desire ; but that night, at any rate, we saw a great company, such as we should like to behold wherever our flag is hoisted, and a great company of the right sort.

Of course, ladies and gentlemen, shopkeepers, and the world-famed keepers of lodging-houses could not deny themselves the treat of hearing Mrs. Booth, even in a circus, for her preaching has always been of such a kind as to attract, charm, and edify people of wealth and taste, while aiming all the while at the humblest intelligence and the roughest of characters. And there were people in the audience who ought to have been in their usual places of worship that night, and who doubtless would have been there had they not known from the memory of previous experiences that Mrs. Booth would speak to them more fearlessly and faithfully and searchingly than their ordinary pastors. Everybody acquainted with Mrs. Booth knows that she hits hard—very hard—at everybody's conscience ; but people who sincerely wish to be right like to be hit hard ; and ministers and others who complain when their people go to submit themselves to the scourge of an evangelist forget that those wounds will prove their healing—the healing of their church as well as of the individuals who are sometimes so severely condemned for running after novelty.

But the vast bulk of the congregation which filled every seat round the great pentagon and in its centre consisted of working people by no means accustomed to any religious service whatsoever. And when every seat had been filled, and standing space, too, occupied below, the passage-way all round the top of the galleries was crowded with a motley throng of young men and lads—fishers of the sea, donkey-drivers of the shore, and what not.

"Oh, dear ! we thought ; no earthly power can keep all those young chaps standing quiet all the time."

Mrs. Booth saw the danger at a glance. The uneasy movement which is inevitable at the first assembling of such a throng was in full progress, when she turned it to a perfect calm by the simple remark—

"We are glad to see you all, and we are sure that, seeing how many people there are who wish to hear, you will be careful not to make a sound which could prevent any one from doing so, unless, indeed, some one should have come in who has neither sense nor conscience, in which case, of course, we cannot expect them to behave themselves, and we shall be forced to ask them to retire."

Not a soul allowed himself to be suspected of answering the dreadful description. For two solid hours those lads stood motionless, gazing at the speaker as intently as the sitting multitude below, and certainly there was enough said that night to make them all look earnestly enough.

It appeared a huge space for a woman's voice to fill, unless, indeed, it had been one of those female preachers whose shrill accents and masculine efforts have brought female ministry so often into contempt.

" I wonder if they can all hear me," said Mrs. Booth to me, when she found how easy it seemed to be to talk in her natural, over-the-table fashion.

" I'll soon find out," I replied ; and, leaving the platform, I passed out at a side entrance and went round to the front one, which was the most distant point from the speaker. There, outside the doors, every word of the lesson could be heard as distinctly as if I had stood within ten feet of the reader, instead of being probably twenty-five yards away. The care bestowed upon the pronunciation of every letter, no less than the desire to make everybody receive every thought, explains in no small degree the pleasure with which huge audiences have invariably listened to Mrs. Booth wherever she has gone.

The sermon I really could not attempt to describe, for, to tell you the honest truth, although naturally addressed in the main to unconverted people, it took hold of me quite as much as everybody else, and I challenge anybody who likes, to try to remember the construction of a sermon which comes from the heart, is aimed at the heart, and reaches its mark.

All I know is, it was about the prodigal son, and that somehow or other the young rascal and his poor old father came about the place and made us all feel uncommonly queer about the throat and eyes. Not that the preacher dressed them in modern apparel, or made them talk street English, as is the fashion with some popular evangelists of the day. She has a marvellous power of presenting the most profound thoughts, and the most remote events, in language which everybody understands, and which is nevertheless as correct and as dignified as the language of scripture itself. She exhibited our heavenly Father's love, and our own base ingratitude, in such a way that one could only feel utter astonishment that anybody could go away that night unsaved.

How fearful was the strain upon the orator's strength no one off the platform could have imagined, so perfectly did she seem at home throughout ; but to one who was near enough to see and feel how every atom of her being was wrapt in the flame of eagerness to save her hearers, it could never be a wonder that her strength should utterly give way beneath such toil. Watches, clocks, signals as to the flight of time were useless to one who could see nothing but perishing souls from the moment she began till the moment she made us all bow to pray; and now all too late we have to mourn that more effectual means were not adopted on this and other occasions to preserve to the world a force so invaluable.

We can only pray and trust that He who is our light and our strength will yet enable Mrs. Booth, and others who are walking in her footsteps, to pour living water on our thirsty land as it flowed that night in the Circus at Hastings.

In May, 1874, a band of converted gipsies, who frequently take services at our stations, were preaching at Portsmouth. We heard that a large circus, at Southampton, was lying entirely unoccupied. It seemed a tempting opportunity to do something for that town, and although we do not, as a rule, hold any service except at our regularly established stations, we ventured upon the experiment. The circus, which held some 3,000 people, was readily secured, and the work began. The town just then was unusually crowded with strangers, awaiting the arrival of the " Malwa," with the remains of Dr. Livingstone.

After the first Sunday, noon-day as well as evening meetings were held, and these were not only blessed and encouraging in themselves, but made the services of the approaching Sabbath widely known.

No one, however, could have anticipated the glorious day that was coming. A thousand people came in the morning, and fifteen hundred in the afternoon. At the close of the latter service, the congregation were invited to follow to an open-air demonstration. Several hundreds did so, and marching in silence for nearly half-an-hour, through the principal streets of the town, they formed up at a place of public resort near the Ordnance House. Of course an immense crowd listened to the addresses delivered, and in the evening the circus was crowded to its utmost capacity.

The evangelist who was leading, and his three gipsy brethren, delivered short, simple, heartfelt and heart-stirring addresses, singing hymns between each address. Every word seemed to go home with the power of the Holy Ghost ; and some two thousand persons remained to the prayer-meeting.

The spirit of prayer seemed to be poured out so abundantly, that it was at first a matter of some difficulty to conduct the meeting with anything like order, without giving offence to many ; but those who wished to engage publicly, were prevailed upon to come near the platform; and so the feeling of the whole meeting was kept concentrated on the soul saving work.

At the first invitation to penitents to come forward, only half a dozen responded to the call ; but as soon as these stood up rejoicing in God, another company came forward. No sooner was the joy of pardon received into the mourners' hearts, than they hastened to seek after others. One young man, about twenty years of age, was overheard praying, immediately after he felt relieved of his guilty load, ' *Please Lord, let me tell somebody, or I shall die."* Upon receiving permission he gladly stood up, and related what God had just done for his soul. This remarkable scene was repeated over and over again. Silent prayer was every now and then requested for some new group of seekers of salvation, whose sobs alone would break the deathly stillness of the building. The marvellous work went on, until the names and addresses had been recorded of ninety-seven persons who had professed to find salvation. The evangelist had closed the meeting over and over again ; but still they came, and now at the last moment, three more came forward, saying " Oh, do stop and pray with us." Their importunity could not be resisted, late as was the hour, and soon the number of the professedly saved was raised to one hundred.

A clergyman and several gentlemen belonging to various

denominations who were assisting to point sinners to Christ, all concurred in saying that they had never known such a time in their lives.

In many instances it was indeed a deliverance out of darkness into light. Whilst they were singing :

> " I the chief of sinners am,
> But Jesus died for me."

a poor woman asked, "Please, sir, did He die *for me ?*" "Oh, yes, that He did," was the reply, and she soon was able to believe as well as to sing it.

A sailor said, "Oh, sir, I came up here with a heavy heart. I am out at sea generally for eleven or twelve months together, and I never have any religious services or anything. But now, praise the Lord, I can go back much lighter. I can go to sea now fearing no storm, for my soul is safe."

Rich as well as poor were found at the feet of Jesus, amongst the sawdust in that circus ring. One gentleman almost ran forward sobbing. He had only landed the night before after four months travel in South America. He said, " I used to spend my Sabbaths in fishing and shooting ; but I praise God for what he has done for my soul now ! " He gave the evangelist his address, and said, " If you can come there, I will take some large hall for your services."

Relatives and friends rejoiced together. A woman said, " My husband and brother have been converted to-night." Another, "Three of my cousins have been saved to-night."

Great was our sorrow when the evangelist, misunderstanding the extent of his discretionary power, returned to London with the news of this glorious day, having closed the series of services, and so let slip the golden opportunity of seizing the town. In our work, as in war, daring disobedience is sometimes the best faithfulness. But we are thankful to know the work did not stop, but was taken up by a gentleman on the spot, and we believe special services

in public buildings have been held at intervals ever
since.

The following description of a Sunday, spent by Mr.
Bramwell Booth and Miss Booth, at the last Theatre we
have taken, shows that the old results follow to-day the old
processes, and that a similar future is assured as far as the
resolution and abilities of a new generation can assure it.

"West Hartlepool, Sunday morning, November 11th. Very
wet, but a good prayer meeting at seven o'clock.

"In the forenoon we turned out into the streets with
some forty in our ring, mostly converted during the month
previous.

"In the afternoon Miss Booth spoke with unusual power,
and a blessed influence was felt by the congregation, which
comfortably filled the pit and first gallery.

"At night, although it was fearfully stormy, the Theatre
was crammed, not less than fifty or sixty people standing
about the pit and stage. Miss Booth preached on 'The
righteous hath hope in his death.' More than half the audience were in tears. While she sang,

> ' Oh, the rocks and the mountains shall all flee away,
> And you shall find a new hiding place that day,'

it seemed to us as though every sinner in the place must
have fled for refuge at once.

"There were soon three long rows of penitents seeking
mercy. One man, in his anxiety to be saved, jumped out of
the pit on to the stage, instead of going round by the regular
steps, and was soon ready to jump for joy.

"Some of the seekers were persuaded to pray aloud for
themselves, and when others heard their cries for mercy,
they too, came forward to seek the Lord.

"About a hundred of us finished up together on the stage
with tears of joy and shouts of triumph, singing—

> ' The opening heavens around me shine
> With beams of sacred bliss.' "

CHAPTER VI.

"DAY BY DAY, WE MAGNIFY THEE."

YES, every day! That is it! The wild whirl of city life is daily carrying the multitude on its thousand eddies to the awful rush and boom of death's terrible waves and to the dark depths of eternity. No day must be lost if anything effective is to be done for the poor dying souls. There are a thousand objects all around to catch every eye and to fill up every mind. The Son of Man cannot be lifted up too often if we are really anxious to have all men drawn unto Him.

And once a man is laid hold of he must not be let go for an evening. A hundred public-house doors must be passed ere he gets home from his work. His home may have little attraction at any time. Since his conversion it may have become a very nest of hornets to him. If you want to make it possible for such a man to get established in the ways of God you must not leave him one leisure evening unprovided for. Reading is not likely to be congenial to him even if he had anywhere to go where such reading as he now takes pleasure in could be done in peace. To open any good book at home is to raise a hullabaloo of ridicule if not of blasphemy which, no matter how valiantly withstood, must render profitable reading impossible. You cannot,

F

must not hope to lead poor people to heaven unless you
lead them *daily.*

More than that ! The man who is daily fought against
must daily fight if he would win, and it makes it unspeakably easier to fight all the working hours alone amongst the
immense majority who oppose, if he can at least fight a few
hours every evening in line with his comrades.

" You were at that ranting-shop last night, then," said
his mate to a man the other day.

" Yes, and I'm going again to-night," was the overwhelming rejoinder, " and I mean to keep on going every day as
long as I live, for God blesses me there."

How much harder it would have been for that man if
days intervened between every attendance at the open-air or
in-door service, and if thus each fresh visit became like a
separate effort with the prospect of new obloquy and difficulty
each time !

But once it is a settled matter that he is coming every
day to help to oppose sin and get other people converted,
the public-house, the club, the social gathering, the worldly
entertainment have lost their chance of catching him. He
has no time for such trifles. They are gone—left behind.
He is " doing a great work and cannot come down."

And in those nightly meetings of his, whether in the
open-air or in-doors, God *does* bless him. It is not that he
can always do or say anything so remarkable for Christ. At
any rate, he again confesses Him before man by his presence.
It is not that he hears such a wonderfully instructive discourse, or gets through any human channel such new or useful teaching, for he may have to come many a night and
hear simple folks like himself who can tell him nothing new,
and who, in fact, address themselves mainly to the unconverted. But he draws nigh to God and God draws nigh to
him, and he goes home with such benefit, with such
strengthening and cheering thoughts as no mere human
teaching could impart.

It is not that he sees anything of a very elevating, refining, or pleasing character, or associates with very extraordinary people. He stands at some ordinary street corner with his brethren ; he enters some plain, humble, undecorated place with but a few perhaps of his own class, or of people even poorer and more ignorant than he himself ; but before he goes home he very likely helps the angels to rejoice over some sinner that repenteth, and the sight of a soul saved gladdens him more than anything else on earth could. He rejoices as if it it were his very own brother, and as one that findeth great spoil.

Scene.—A street in Whitechapel, 10.30 p.m. Two men approaching each other, their faces shining all over alike.

" Well, brother, how are you ? "

" Happy, bless the Lord, we've just had four souls at S——"

" We've only had two ; but they were good'uns. I think one of them was a mate of ——'s, but he got nicely through."

" Hallelujah ! " " Bless the Lord."

" Good night." " Good night."

" But what about their wives and families if they're out so late ? " Bless you, the wife of this one was there with her baby, too, till nine o'clock. And when she wanted to go home, she did not ask her husband to leave that blessed prayer-meeting till the poor gasping sinner was happy in Jesus. Never such a thing ! She would rather he had stopped there all night.

" We can't both get out at night," says another, " so we take it turn about to mind the children."

" My husband is very good. Though he won't come himself, he never hinders me from coming as often as I like," says another woman, whose husband is still unconverted.

To people whose home only contains the necessaries of physical existence—to whom a library is as uninteresting as

the shelves that bear it—whose earthly ideas are bounded
by a very narrow circle—who are far too weary every night
with their daily toil to enter upon any new labour which
does not bring the energy it demands back to them in
enjoyment at once—to such people an evening at home
alone would be, comparatively speaking, a dull and useless
one.   An evening in the company of their companions on
the way to heaven is far more refreshing and beneficial every
way.   Not that home and children do not demand the most
sacred and painstaking care ; but if home and children are
not all snug by seven or eight o'clock at night, they. are
never likely to be so, and we make our services thus late to
suit the convenience of the people.

A servant girl has the option of a day out once a month,
or an evening per week.   She chooses the weekly evening,
and rides two miles to be at the open-air and indoor services.
"I haven't been home for weeks,". she says.   Her friends
are all unconverted.   To visit them is to run into danger.
Christ is more than father, mother, sister, or brother to her,
and she will only call a little while before service time now
and then on a Sunday to invite them to come along.   "And
if mother does come, I'm determined she shall hear me pray
for her before them all."   She will get all her family yet, we
believe.

The Mission having found out the need of the people, has,
therefore, from the first laid down the law "An open-air
service and an in-door service—at least one of each—at every
station, every night, if possible."   Of course, it is not always
possible to hold an open-air service ; and it is not always
possible to hold one open to the public in-doors, seeing that
meetings of a more private kind must occupy the only
building we have to use.   Of course, every evangelist
employed by the Mission has not had the strength needed
for so many services—some, alas! have not had the diligence
either.   These last have soon found that, as there was a way
into the Mission, there was also a way out.   Of course, the

members at every small station have not been able to muster
every night in sufficient strength to carry on an open-air
meeting ; at times, also, their leaders have caused them to
err in dealing with a slack hand, and leaving undone the
things that ought to be done.

If an evangelist feels that he must be up and doing for
his Master every day ; that he cannot, dare not, let a day
pass without winning as many souls as he possibly can,
ought not all whom that evangelist teaches to feel just as he
does ? And if the number of those who thus bear about
daily the burden of souls continually increases, how can they
all be faithful to their convictions unless the number of
services is continually increasing proportionately ?

But another argument for the multiplication of daily
work seems quite as weighty. Walk through even one
district of any city. Look at the miles and miles of working
people's homes, street after street, row after row. If the
object be to make all these people hear the word of God, how
many services must be held nightly to bring the sound to
every door even once a month ? " But may the people not all
be reached by standing near some of the main thoroughfares ? " Oh, no, not directly, at any rate. The men may,
perhaps, to a large extent ; but not the women. To reach
these the Gospel must be proclaimed near enough to every
door for the words to be distinctly heard through the
windows. Oh, what a work is still to be done ! Lord God,
who is sufficient for these things ?

But daily service is not a mere Mission question. Who-
ever invented a religion without daily attendance on public
divine service ? Why, the devil, of course, whose policy
always has been, is, and will be, as long as he has to deal
with sinful mortals, to persuade them to put off till to-morrow
what they should do to-day !

Did not our fathers eat manna in the wilderness, and stand
before the tabernacle of God every day ? Did not God
institute daily service in His temple ? Did not the Psalmist

find it his only desire to dwell in the house of the Lord all the days of his life ? Did not the holy people before Christ was manifested meet daily in the Temple ? Did not He, our Master and our Example, daily teach the people, and daily in the Temple, when near enough to Jerusalem ? Did not His apostles daily in the synagogues, and from house to house, preach, and teach, and heal ? Ay, did not every converted reader of these pages so understand and practise every day religion in the time of their first love ?

" Oh, but that was in a time of special services."

No doubt; and may God awaken the holders of special services to the solemn responsibility involved in practically demonstrating that they can, when they choose to make the effort, attend to God's work daily, and yet then of leaving it unattended to on most week days for the rest of the year !

" But I don't feel to need service every day. I have a life which is not dependent on services for its maintenance."

" And what about your neighbours who have no such life ? Should not your enjoyment of it make you daily more anxious to bring them into it ? "

" Well, I really don't see that, looking at the claims of business, and family, and one's own mind and soul, so much can really be expected of *everyone* ; of course there may be people who feel called to it ; but I don't."

" This persuasion cometh not of Him that calleth *you* to glory and to virtue."

There is neither glory nor virtue in deserting the service of the Lord and the salvation of men for days together. If people do not serve the Lord daily in public, it is simply because their everyday life has very little of the heavenly about it.

The love of a living daily-interceding Saviour, no less than the iniquities and woes of a dying world, call for daily labour in the great vineyard, such as can only be performed in bands ; and if the Judge coming in such an hour as we think not, finds our place of worship shut and us sitting at home, what then? "*Blessed* is that servant whom his Master when He cometh shall find *so* doing?"

While striving, however, to keep holy every day in the year, and to make the most of every leisure hour for the salvation of souls, the Mission of course finds Sunday its spiritual market day. The following description of a Sunday at one of the smallest stations, will convey some idea of the way in which the day is utilized generally.

There is a prayer-meeting at seven in the morning, an open-air service from ten till eleven, in-door service eleven to twelve-thirty, open-air again from two to three, in-door service, generally an experience meeting from three till half-past four, after which a plain tea is provided, at cost price, for those who prefer to keep together preparatory to the evening's work. A prayer-meeting is held after tea, concluded in time to get to the open-air stand at six o'clock. The in-door service at seven o'clock with the prayer-meeting, which forms its great practical feature, rarely concludes before ten o'clock. Such is a Christian Mission Sunday.

At large stations, of course, a number of open-air services are held simultaneously on Sunday evenings, and in some cases at earlier hours also, in order fully to utilize all the available force, and occasionally the whole of the Sunday morning or afternoon is spent out of doors.

We need scarcely say that, in many cases, our people have to walk a considerable distance to each service, so that really an efficient Mission evangelist or member has, with the exception of an hour or two for meals, some fifteen hours "on duty" every Sabbath. And the people who delight in such days of rest, used to be unwilling to listen to anything about religion! Surely something has happened which it would puzzle the men of science, and the Sunday League to account for!

It is difficult to explain to any stranger the eagerness with which Mission people hasten to any service they can attend; the reluctance with which they go away, the seemingly exhaustless energy thrown into the work. The following lines from a favourite Mission song will convey a pretty fair idea of the state of feeling from which all this springs.

> Oh! the Christian Mission is a grand device,
> 　　Glory Hallelujah.
> For turning this earth into paradise,
> 　　Sing glory Hallelujah.
>
> 　　Chorus—Hallelujah, Glory Hallelujah!
> 　　　　　　Hallelujah, Glory Hallelujah!
> 　　　　　　Hallelujah to the Lamb,
> 　　　　　　Sing, Glory Hallelujah.
>
> They said it was only a flash in the pan,
> But the flash a glorious fire began.
>
> We go to the deepest in the mire,
> For we love to pull them out of the fire.
>
> We lead them to our pardoning God,
> And the brands are quenched in Jesu's blood.
>
> The worst have had their sins forgiven,
> And found on earth the days of heaven.
>
> In the streets, in the lanes, aye, anywhere,
> Our Cathedral is the open air.
>
> We may be rough, and speak aloud,
> But our words are blessed to the hardened crowd.
>
> Yes, saving souls is our delight,
> Whether 'tis morning, noon, or night.
>
> Many who once fought by our side
> Have won the fight, and crossed the tide.
>
> From suffering, want, disease, and pain,
> They've gone with Jesus Christ to reign.
>
> We grasped their hands in Jordan's flood,
> And they shouted, " Victory through the Blood."
>
> No learning, money, or friends, we boast,
> But on our side is the heavenly host.
>
> We're soldiers fighting for our God,
> And we shall conquer through the blood.
>
> And when our work in the Mission is o'er,
> We'll meet and sing on Canaan's shore.
>
> And of all we've seen, or hope to see,
> We give the glory, Lord, to thee!

CHAPTER VII.

HOW WE SING.

WE have a great deal of reason to sing, have we not? Yes, and we sing a great deal. Our people are very fond of singing, and it is well that they are so, for singing helps them over many a rough piece of their rugged pathway, and through many a season of darkness and trial; and not only is the singing blessed to the singers, but, thank God, it is used, more perhaps than anything else, to attract the people to our services.

Not that our singing is peculiarly attractive from an artistic point of view. We doubt whether to people of taste and musical education it might not be rather repulsive than otherwise. Such a friend once aptly called it "a joyful noise unto the Lord." We are quite prepared to admit that our singing, especially in the open air, may more closely resemble the blare of a military band than the melody of the sanctuary; but if the people who sing and the people who hear like such singing—prefer it, in fact, to any other—what then?

"Educate and elevate their tastes."

And what in the meantime?

"Oh, break them of the other by degrees."

But how if they show a disposition to sing more and

more loudly and energetically the longer they walk in the new happy path, and if they keep gathering other noisy singers into their ranks?

We should like somebody to try teaching our people a more refined style of singing; or, rather, we should not like it to be tried, because we find that the sound and force of the singing is in exact proportion to the amount and character of the life existing anywhere amongst us. And a moment's consideration shows that this must be so.

Our training-classes are held in the tap-room, the public-house free-and-easy saloon, the low concert-hall, the fore-castle, and the barrack-room. From these classic neigh-bourhoods we draw our singers, who, the moment they become "glad in the Lord," feel an irresistible inclination to sing more loudly than ever they did before.

Anyone who has listened to the sounds that are borne on the midnight air from the open windows of the public-house, mingled with the squeak of the violin and the rattle of mugs and pots, or to the not less boisterous hilarity of the waggon-loads of holiday-makers who rush through the streets on Mondays and holidays, must be aware that when the working-classes are "enjoying themselves" according to their notions, their forceful lungs have the freest play. How much more, then, when these same people are overflowing with a joy they never dreamt of before, must they be expected to give vent to it according to their strength?

Given the largest number of these people in one place— given the most numerous and frequent accessions to the company, the most numerous and frequent victories, the greatest cause for rejoicing, and you have inevitably the greatest noise. Such is our experience, at any rate.

We shall not further plead for this sort of singing as it concerns the singers, simply because it seems to us the only singing possible to them. When they begin to lose their taste for it, they are losing their taste for singing, and for lively, happy, powerful religion altogether. Such is our invariable experience.

But as to the effects of this singing, let facts speak.

"The singing of the procession, and the march back to the station, seemed to us extraordinarily full of zest and power. It was quite amusing to notice the puzzled look on the face of some street musicians, who continued to strike their instruments, though they could scarcely have heard them at all themselves, as we swept by singing

> ' I love Jesus, Hallelujah,
> I love Jesus, yes, I do ;
> I love Jesus, He's my Saviour ;
> Jesus smiles and loves me too.' "

"But what good does it all do ? "

The landlady of a public-house said one day, " Who are these men and women who sing and preach in our street ? "

" They are the Christian Mission."

" If they would not sing in our street I would give them ten shillings and would contribute to the work, for they are singing and preaching all my best customers away from me."

" But," replies her informant, an old customer, " *we* can afford to give the Christian Mission more than that *now*. We are converted to God. We have happy homes, happy wives, happy children, and money to spare."

A young man, the son of a widowed mother, living in a country village, was led away by drink and evil companions, going from bad to worse, until at length, on a drunken spree, he left his cottage home and his poor broken-hearted mother, whose gray hairs he was fast bringing to the grave, and went all unknown to her to Cardiff. Here he signed articles for sea ; but just before his ship left the port he heard our people singing in the open air, and was induced to follow to the hall, where, deeply convinced of sin, he sought and found mercy. How his first letter home must

have gladdened the poor widow's heart and made *her sing*
for joy !

One evening, in a densely-populated neighbourhood, a
band of people were heard singing—

> "Stop, poor sinner, stop and think
> Before you farther go;
> Can you sport upon the brink
> Of everlasting woe ?
> Hell beneath is gaping wide,
> Vengeance waits the dread command
> Soon to stop your sport and pride
> And sink you with the damned.
>
> Once again I charge you—Stop !
> For unless you warning take,
> 'Ere you are aware you'll drop
> Into the burning lake."

A solemn warning, sung in a way that must have convinced everyone that it was *meant!* A poor woman who
had long been living in sin, heard, and could not forget it.
So powerfully did the Spirit of God apply the words to her
conscience, that she said she " could not sleep at night, nor
rest by day." She decided, as so many have done before,
to try to get rid of the painful impression by " change of
air and scene." But it was no use. Early in the morning
at the booking-office, " Once again I charge you—Stop," rang
in her ears above all the bustle and the whistling of the
engines. " Once again I charge you—Stop ! " seemed to
come sweeping down upon her on the breeze as she sat on
the steamboat helplessly asking herself, " How can I ? "
" Once again I charge you—Stop ! " was all she could hear or
think of in the great city to which she journeyed, day after
day, and night after night, and the terrible charge fell upon
her heart with increasing weight every day, until at last,
upon her return home, she did stop. She found the last
lines of that outspoken hymn delightfully true as she fell
broken-hearted at the feet of Jesus—

" None who come shall be denied—
He says there still is room."

A sailor who had just come into port and drawn his
money was on his way to a place of amusement when the
singing in a little hall arrested him. He stood for awhile to
listen outside. The music was just " his sort of thing,"
though the words were entirely " out of his line." By and
by he ventured into the lobby, and then curiosity to see the
people who could sing religion so merrily drew him inside.
A hymn-book was put into his hand, and he was invited to
a front seat. He thought the singing so " very lively" that
he said to himself, " I will stop and hear what they have
to say."

And then God spoke to him, laying bare all the secrets of
his past life so forcibly that he resolved there and then to
give up drink at any rate. He was reminded that this was
not enough, but said he would come again and hear more.

" What's to pay ? " he naturally inquired, unaccustomed
to hear singing, or meet with any sort of accommodation
ashore, without paying dearly for it.

" Nothing to pay," was the surprising reply, and the next
evening he was one of the first to accept our hospitality
again.

This time allusion was made by the speaker to a mother's
prayers, and the sailor prodigal's heart was broken. Many
a year had his poor mother prayed for him while he had
been drinking and running to every excess of riot with bad
companions. He had stood by her death-bed, and her entreaties that he would give up sin and meet her in heaven
had so far moved him that he promised to comply with her
wishes, and was serious for a time. But, alas, " the drink
again " did its terrible work. All was forgotten, and he
plunged into sin as madly as ever, till thus marvellously
brought face to face with his mother's God.

Now, with tearful eyes, he asked, "Can I be converted ? "
and, falling on his knees, sought forgiveness in right-down

earnest. When peace and pardon flooded his soul with rapturous joy, who can wonder that he could not suppose all this great benefit was to cost nothing, and repeated the question of the night before—

"What's to pay?"

"Nothing to pay," was again the answer of course, and he went away exclaiming—

"Well, well! a teetotaler and converted, and nothing to pay!"

A wretched drunkard sat one Sunday morning upon his doorstep with parched lips and aching head, waiting, as so many thousands, alas! do, for the opening hour of *their* church—the public-house—his own house a wreck, and his family as miserable as his continual ill-conduct could make them. As he sat there a band of strong men suddenly came round the street corner, singing—

> "Oh, you must be a lover of the Lord,
> Or you can't go to heaven when you die."

Before he could raise himself up to get into the house they were standing right opposite, and what surprised him most was to see two old mates amongst the throng.

What must have been his emotion when one of them, showing him to everybody, said :

"There is a man sitting on this doorstep that I have drunk gallons of ale with at the "Red Lion," and he will tell you what a character I have been ; but now, thank God, I am converted, and have joined the Christian Mission."

"The Lord will save you too. Come and go with us," added the speaker, looking his old friend straight in the face. The poor fellow looked at his converted mate's clothes, and at his own, and the contrast between them seemed to say with a loud voice, "Religion is better than drunkenness," an unanswerable argument which seemed to press itself upon him more and more as the day wore on, in spite of all that he could do to turn his attention to something more agreeable.

In the evening a band of singers came along again, this time with,

> " We are bound for the land of the pure and the holy,
>> The home of the happy, the kingdom of love,
> Ye heart-burdened ones who in misery languish,
>> Oh, say, will you go to the Eden above ? "

Heart-burdened enough, the poor fellow, brushing away a tear, cried, " Give me my hat. I'll gang wi' them chaps." Slinking along behind, he sat down, as he supposed, in a quiet corner of the theatre to which they led him. There were his mates right on the stage, and when they rose and sang, to the tune of " Annie Lisle " the verse,

> " Earth hath many a scene of sorrow,"

he said. " Ah, Bill, that's true, for I have just left one." Every hymn struck him with overwhelming force. " As for the man that preached," he said, " he must have known all about my life. Somebody has been doing me a good turn again in telling that fellow all he knows."

The prayer meeting commenced with the hymn,

> "With a sorrow for sin let repentance begin,
>> Then conversion of course will draw nigh,
> But, till washed in the blood
> Of a crucified Lord,
>> We shall never be ready to die."

While this was being sung, his two mates had found him out, and began to urge him to seek salvation at once. " I can bear it no longer," he said, and took his great load to the great Sin-bearer, who gave him at once the relief he needed, so that he could say, " I know and feel I am changed man. Glory be to God in the highest ! "

" You sing hymns to song tunes ? " Yes we do, and that systematically and purposely, not merely because the song

tunes are the most lively and popular, and in every way the
best we can find ; but because the mere fact of using a song
tune is calculated in itself to help us in our one great object
—" to catch men."

A stranger stood outside one of our halls one evening in
utter amazement. A goodly company of people were singing, and evidently singing with great enjoyment too. The
tune was that of " Auld lang syne."

"Whatever are they singing ? " asked the stranger.
There was no mistake about the tune, but not one word of
the song ! He could not for some minutes fairly realize,
however, that these were religious people actually singing
solemn earnest truth to these familiar notes. " Well, I
never heard such a thing in my life," he naturally remarked,
when he fully comprehended what was going on, and just
such a surprise has led, we are sure, thousands upon thousands of people to stay and hear, in the open air, or indoors,
what we have got to say.

We do not think that the old-fashioned prejudice against
the use of any sort of music in religious work, has many
surviving representatives, but should this page meet the eye
of one, let us just say one word in defence of the practice.

Suppose a man or a woman who has persistently kept
away from any religious influence, hears the grand old
chorus—

> " I do believe, I will believe
> That Jesus died for me :
> That on the cross He shed His blood
> From sin to set me free."

And suppose the last line especially, repeated again and
again, and again, impresses him with the fact so long lost
sight of, that God cares so much about delivering him from
the bondage he is under, that he sacrificed his only son to
buy him this freedom. Will the angels who note the good
impression made, and perchance the dawnings of repentance
in the poor wanderer's heart, be any the less pleased if the

repetition of those great words was occasioned by the use of the tune of " Auld Lang Syne ? "

Should we be thought irreverent if we ventured to doubt, whether angels are not too much occupied with greater thoughts to notice whether the tune be " The Old Hundred," " Ring the Bell Watchman," or " Wait for the Waggon," supposing them to know the difference between the three ?

Would it not be a very hazardous thing to attempt to determine the proportion of demi-semi-quavers to minims in the songs of the better land ? (*They* are always called " songs.")

But without troubling the angels, we venture to say that not one of our readers, if they could see and hear the happy people who used to be so dark and wretched not long since, would cavil at their joy, because it is expressed in the merriest of melodies.

" When we were in town," said a country friend, by no means disposed by his tastes to adopt our sort of music, " we looked in at your place in——"

" Well, and what did you think of the singing ? "

" Oh they sang like troopers, and when we got out—— kept singing the tune over all the rest of our walk."

It is by no means the least satisfactory piece of work done in 1876, to have put in print the music and words of our hymns, and we would say to any who do not find it easy to reconcile this sort of singing to their taste or their notions of religious propriety, " Will you try their effect upon the children, or the poor ? "

Is it not the most natural idea in the world, when you wish to show working people that religion will suit them, to fit its songs to the tunes they are fondest of ? At anyrate one, as we think unanswerable argument is, that the plan *succeeds*.

A young man who recently had a mission man for a fellow lodger, said to the landlady as he came downstairs, worried by the words the other had been singing in their

bed-room, " What's up with our mate ?   He must be going
mad ; and I wish he was out on it."

The poor sinner went to his work ; but soon another
young man broke out by his side, singing one of those songs
which stamp the mission man everywhere.   Turning upon
the singer indignantly, he said, " What ! have you joined
those folks, too ? "

" Yes," was the rejoinder, " and you would make a good
soldier too."

"No, never ! " answered the rebel ; but he was soon in
the ranks, no doubt as ready as the rest to take up the song

> "Oh, I'm glad I'm in this army,
> Yes, I'm glad I'm in this army:
> And I'll battle for the Lord."

And so long as the Mission people go on fighting and
conquering, will any one really complain of the music they
march to ?   Surely not.

CHAPTER VIII.

COMMUNION OF SAINTS.

"WE know that we have passed from death unto life, because we love the brethren," is a rule which we see continually exemplified in connection with our services.

The new convert, if not, indeed, the stranger who ventures within our gates, is immediately ushered into a family circle where everyone feels the tenderest interest in everyone else, and where no stiffness, introduction, or formality can for a moment be tolerated. Something more than the familiarity of the workshop; something more like the jovial good-fellowship of the tap-room, purified and elevated by spiritual influence; this is the kind of atmosphere in which the convert suddenly finds more than compensation for the loss of godless friends and companions in sin.

The love of the people for one another demands and finds expression in a multitude of gatherings of a socially-religious kind where, to an extent impossible in more public services, they "have fellowship one with another."

" Come near, all ye that fear God, and I will declare what He hath done for my soul," modernized in our favourite song—

> " Come ye that fear the Lord unto me,
> I've something good to say
> About the narrow way;
> For Christ the other day saved my soul "

is a cry constantly heard amongst us, and always heartily responded to.

Meetings for the relation of religious experience are held, as a rule, once every Lord's day, generally in the afternoon, sometimes, as a variation from preaching, in the evening. These meetings are open to the public, and have been used to the salvation of many.

At the older stations, where there are disciples of several years' standing, the relations of experience are frequently full, and marvellous in their heavenly height and depth. Where only young converts and speakers abound, and indeed, as a rule, everywhere, short, sometimes very short, speaking prevails.

As an example of the rapidity with which people burning with first love manage to declare what God has done for them, we may cite a meeting, thus described by the evangelist who conducted it :

" Sixty-six men and women spoke, we sang ten times, one man had a fit, one woman fainted, and the benediction was pronounced in sixty-seven minutes, and we went home praising God."

But what *can* people say at such a speed ? The following is a pretty fair representation of what was said by various persons on such occasions :

No. 1.—" Friends, I am washed in the blood of the Lamb."

No. 2.—" The last ten weeks have been the happiest of my life."

No. 3.—" I mean to live better next year than ever I did in my life."

No. 4.—" I want two things during the coming year : I want to feel every second the cleansing blood on me, and the Spirit of God dwelling within. I feel the blood is on me now, cleansing from all sin, and that God is within, giving me the victory."

No. 5.—" I promised God and Brother D—— last watch-night that I would speak to someone about their souls every day during the year, and, bless God ! I have, and I have the names of forty of them who have been converted."

No. 6.—" I am saved outside and in."

No. 7.—" This has been a memorable year in my history. On the 16th of July I asked God to pardon my sins, and He did it. Last Sunday He saved my wife, and, bless God, I can now say—

" Here I give my all to Thee,
Time and friends and earthly store."

I had heard the passing-bell tolling this morning for some-one who had died very suddenly, and I said if that had been me I should have gone straight to heaven."

No. 8.—" Thank God, though I have been a great sinner, I have found a great Saviour. I 've been a rough un. I could punch and box a bit ; but now I fight for Jesus, for He has washed away all my sins."

No. 9.—" My feet are on the rock. I have been trying to work for Jesus. I am unworthy, but God help me ! "

No. 10.—" He has saved me and saved my wife, and we are going on to heaven together."

No. 11.—" I'm a soldier for Jesus, and am winning vic-tories over self."

No. 12.—" By the grace of God I am saved."

No. 13.—" This has been a month of weakness, but I think I have lived nearer to God."

No. 14.—" I am happy, and my wife is happy. I love the Lord Jesus. He makes me happy. I had a good old father I promised to meet in heaven, and now I am on the way."

No. 15.—" I am fully saved and happy in God."

No. 16.—" And, thank God ! I'm saved and washed in the blood of the Lamb. I am going on."

No. 17.—" I am saved."

No. 18.—" I am clinging to the Cross,"

No. 19.—"I can truly say—

> ' Nothing on earth do I desire
> But Thy pure love within my breast ;
> This, only this, I will require,
> And freely give up all the rest.' "

No. 20.—"I am glad I am washed in the blood of the Lamb."

No. 21.—" We often forget to praise God for the Mission. I hear its praise wherever I go. I go four miles off daily, and I hear of it there. I thank God for this. I praise God for what I have received through it. I never forget to pray for it when I'm talking to God, for if the Lord had not sent it here, I should not have been on my way to heaven."

No. 22.—"I can praise the Lord that He has kept me faithful—praise God that there ever was a Mission that spoke to me and led me to Christ, and trust the Lord will yet give me health and strength to push on the good work."

No. 23.—"I have had a long illness, but the Lord has brought me through. I am surrounded by ungodly people, but He has kept me faithful. Oh ! may He give me and give us all grace to see what stones we may throw in the way of others ! May we not be a hindrance to anyone !"

No. 24.—" Praise God that He found me out and followed me up. Most of us were led and brought in, and difficulties were cleared out of our way. Praise the Lord, He has cleared away mine ! The Lord bless us all ! "

No. 25.—" I do bless God for what Jesus has done for me. I'm trusting in Him every day. He is a very present help in the time of trouble. I have never been so happy as I have been since I came to Him. Bless the Lord for the Mission work! I should like to do more for Him."

No. 26.—" Praise God that He ever found me out with the singing. I heard it one night outside Brother ——'s house, when it was pouring with rain. They were praying when I went in, and I have been trusting in Jesus ever since. May

the Lord keep me on ! I hope we shall see the room full.
If I can only bring one in I will. Sinners can see I never
was so happy before."

No. 27.—"I feel thankful the Mission was ever drawn to
lift up the standard of the Cross, for I was in the wrong
road till it met my sight. The Lord give me wisdom, for I
desire to give a hand in this great work ! I pray in faith.
I am very thankful for a place amongst you and in the
Gospel ship. The Lord help me to move on and keep
us all ! "

No. 28.—"Bless the Lord ! I have been trusting in Him
four years. I was under conviction for seven years. I've
been round the world three times, but I never had one
minute's peace till I gave my soul to Jesus, four years ago,
when I came to the penitent form. I know the place where
the Lord saved me. I have had trouble since then. One of
my arms is paralyzed, and I thought it a great trouble at the
time, but the Lord has blessed it all to me. And though 1
have had a great deal of persecution and abuse for Jesus'
sake, they wouldn't get me to give Him up for anything."

No. 29.—"The Lord has seemed to say to me, ' Feed my
sheep !—feed my lambs ! ' and I have done it, with the
Lord's help. Sometimes I think ' a prophet is not without
honour, save in his own country ; ' but I will testify for the
Lord as long as He lends me breath. Sometimes the devil
says, ' Turn it up,' but then there comes a knock at the
door, and in comes some seeking soul and finds peace ; and,
therefore, I can say I am very glad to see them under the
roof. My inmost desire is still to work for the Master, and
when I look back and see what has been done the last
twelvemonths, I can praise the Lord ! "

The last speaker was formerly one of the most hopeless
drunkards in this neighbourhood. He is now, as he so
beautifully expressed, " a father in Israel."

No. 30.—"I am glad I am saved, I know I am saved."

No. 31.—"I can say with a clear conscience that all my

sins are pardoned. I have had six weeks of it, bless the
Lord."

No. 32.—"I feel I am nearer to God than ever I was
before."

No. 33.—"Well, I praise God that I know my sins are
forgiven. I have been saved a week."

No. 34.—"I am so glad Jesus saves me now. It's the
best week I ever had."

No. 35.—"Jesus has done so much for me, I must
speak."

No. 36.—"It is impossible to tell how much joy I have."

No. 37.—"Glory be to God, I have at last been able to
move! For a long time I lived in Grumbling Street, but now
have got into Thanksgiving Square. Is there anyone here
would like to change? There's a house to let; come and
live next door to me."

No. 38.—Says she wants more pluck, so that she might
do more work for the Lord in the open-air as well as
inside.

No. 39.—Says he is very happy indeed since the Lord
has saved him. He thinks it a fine thing to be a Christian,
his joy being a deal greater than ever his sorrow was. "Oh,
bless the Lord for ever taking in such a wretch as me!
Before I heard you preach I was a rank Atheist."

No. 40.—Says she knows she is on the right side, and in
spite of anyone else she is going to stick to Jesus. Although
people do say she is going wrong, she does not mean to be
beaten by Satan. She means to beat him.

No. 41.—An infant in Jesus, says she is almost overwhelmed sometimes with joy (or swelling of the heart, as
she puts it).

No. 42.—Says he can talk best about his Jesus when quiet
at home; but it makes him shake in public.

No. 43.—Says he likes to get the steam up at home, then
when he gets to the meeting to turn the tap on fully, and
set the engine going; he likes plenty of steam!

No. 44.—" Oh, my blessed Jesus, what would I have done without Him when I was left to battle with this cold world alone ? Oh, bless Him ! How I do love Him !"

No. 45.—Says he counted the cost, and after putting all together, he found to be a Christian was profitable for this life. It was the means of filling his pockets as well as his soul.

No. 46.—" Oh, praise the Lord ! I can boast of having a clean heart. For a long time I have wanted to serve the Lord fully, and now I mean to follow all the way."

No. 47.—" To-day has been a good day to my soul. If it's so sweet to live here with and for Jesus, what must it be to be there, where all are holy ? "

No. 48.—Thinks it a blessed religion. It is so cheap, or he, with a large family to support, could never have bought it. For six weeks he has almost lived in heaven.

No. 49.—" Why talk about heaven ! I find it's heaven all the way to heaven."

No. 50.—" Friends, I'm not *half* saved, not *a bit* saved, I am saved all over. I had been ten years a poor prodigal, and I was a drunkard, a swearer, a blackguard, and everything that is bad, but now me and my wife are going to heaven."

In order to understand why such speaking never loses its interest and freshness, the reader must endeavour to add in imagination to the above words the idea of new converts rising up week by week amidst the joyous shouts of many to give us their novel testimony, and must fill up the scene with shining faces, flashing eyes, bursts of merry song, words and tunes so familiar to most of those present that a verse needs only to be commenced without any warning by one to be taken up in a moment and sung with the heartiness and vigour of a carousal by all, flowing tears, rough, open-mouthed strangers at the back drinking in every word with utter astonishment, until a dirty hand goes up with a sudden jerk to one cheek or the other, or the sad face sinks down on to the bench in front, while rejoicing saints crowd around to pray for the poor sinner who sobs and cries for mercy.

Just one example of the marvellous effect which God's Spirit constantly gives to half a dozen simple words let fall by one or another at these meetings.

"It was an experience meeting one Sabbath afternoon. A large number got up and testified for Jesus. Among them was our dear Brother ——. He spoke of the peace and joy that he had in believing, and I think I see him as he stood in the midst of the hall and looked around upon us all, saying, with quivering lips and beaming eye, 'I've got it—I've got it! My ticket's safe. I'm all right, ready-packed up. And, oh, dearly-beloved friends, have you obtained peace? If you have not, never rest short of it, for I can assure you that you will never be really happy till you have yielded yourself and all you have to Him.' Well, those words sank deep down into my heart. But I was proud—I was stubborn.

"At last I could stand it no longer. I went home into the country. It was a lovely summer's day; the birds were singing sweetly, the flowers were blooming, and all nature was smiling on every hand. But I was sad. I looked up-ward, and the scalding tears came thickly. I thought, oh how I did so wish that God had pardoned *me*, that *I* was accepted in the beloved. Something said, 'Why not be sure to-day? Why not make sure now? Why not this very moment? Kneel down and ask for your assurance. You can have it for asking for, as well as Brother——.' But I could not kneel in the road. Dear reader, you will smile, I know, but when a soul is in reality seeking after Jesus, it will do anything to find Him. Well, there was a field of wheat close by. Something said, 'Get in among the wheat.' I did so, and fell upon my knees while the corn was waving and rustling around, and if I never prayed in all my life before, I did then. I told the Lord that I would not rise from my knees nor leave the spot, until He gave me the sense of sin forgiven, my ticket for glory, my title clear.

"And oh, bless the Lord, oh my soul! I had not knelt there long before the Saviour showed His lovely face. Promise after promise came into my mind. I heard by faith the words, 'Thy sins *are* forgiven thee—go in peace.' 'I have called thee by thy name—thou art mine.' I was happy, my soul was filled with joy unspeakable, and full of glory, and ever after that, I could shout and sing of redeeming love, and never tire of praising my Lord and King."

At smaller meetings of this sort, held on various week nights, the leader, an experienced disciple, has the opportunity not only of hearing all, but of giving to all, either one by one or collectively, as he thinks best, advice with regard to every day religion. The course of procedure at these family gatherings is continually varied, the only permanent feature of them being the universal effort to "bear one another's burdens, and so fulfil the law of Christ."

It is an inevitable consequence of the intense friendship of the people for one another, that tea-drinking should be very popular amongst them. And why should they not have frequent tea-meetings, provided they pay for them? A free tea is certainly a method of gathering together many who could in no other way be induced to come and listen to the gospel of Christ. But we look with great doubt and little hope upon crowds who come to seek the bread that perisheth, and who even when the Master himself dispensed it, generally went away unchanged spiritually. The Mission has reaped some glorious fruit from free teas, and will doubtless do so upon many occasions yet to come, but it does not pretend to supply its converts with tea gratis. We look with the greatest suspicion upon congregations kept together by such means, and upon movements which continually afford to able-bodied men and women, the opportunity to feed upon the bounty of others. No, no! a company of working people are perfectly well able, unless in times of extraordinary distress, and perfectly glad if their *hearts* are set upon it, to provide themselves with victuals, tables and crockery, and to load (and unload) the tables well, at their own expense. Nay more, upon a pinch, working people can get up, by clubbing their own means and getting help from their trades-folk friends, a subscription tea, all the provisions gratis, and so much a head for everybody who sits down to pay as well. At Stockton and Middlesbro' where so many of the converts are iron workers earning good wages, such teas have been provided for 1,000 and 850 people respectively, the tables being given chiefly by friendly tradespeople or employers, who see the value of the work, and a shilling being charged to each tea-drinker. Commonly enough the poor themselves supply humbler tables, all comers to which pay sixpence.

By such means many a struggle to make stations self-supporting is made easy, and after tea many of our happiest and most useful meetings have been held. Friends, relatives, neighbours, workmates are often induced to " take a ticket," and come to such a meeting, little imagining how much warmer than the tea will be the loving spiritual influence, which will surround, and pervade, and overwhelm them after the tables are cleared away. Large public meetings, comprising people from various localities, seem scarcely possible without the social cup, and such meetings, in addition to the salvation of souls, have a most useful effect in bringing together and encouraging those who, perhaps, in much smaller companies, and under vastly different circum-stances, have daily to carry on the great warfare wherein all so greatly delight.

And, besides, provision must be made for the enjoyment of holidays. Mission people want no " entertainments." They gave up all that sort of thing when they gave God all their heart. And, if any of them were to become so changed for the worse as to desire anything of the kind, we trust the Mission will never sink so low as to provide it. There are plenty of people to supply entertainments such as the worldly will gladly attend. We have a higher calling. We must work the work of Him that sent us while it is day, for the night cometh wherein no man can work.

" But may not men be kept from the public-house by such means ? "

Undoubtedly they may ; but what then ?

" Well, it is a first step in the right direction."

Certainly ; but we do not find it a step which makes the steps to the cross more easy of ascent. Rather the contrary, for to-day, as some time since, we find " the publicans and harlots " stepping into the kingdom of heaven much more frequently than the orderly sinners who " do no one any harm," " do their best," and " keep themselves and their families respectable." There are instances, over which we will always rejoice, in which reformation is followed by repentance ; but they are far too rare to make it pay the Mission miner to work the entertainment " vein," while the Gospel of Christ simply set forth, without the expense or trouble of a careful " get-up," is sure, any one evening, to do a far deeper, grander, surer work upon the heart and conscience of somebody. And that is not all. If, in getting up and going through an " entertainment," the spiritual life of one convert is injured, his taste for purely heavenly things impaired, his solemn earnest view of the fearful realities of the sinner's future laughed into dimness, his hold upon his God slackened, his continual spirit of prayer and faith and his ceaseless readiness to take part in spiritual exercises broken in upon, a mischief is done which, perhaps, many a night's toil and prayer will not repair. Therefore, the Mission cannot and will not have anything to do with entertainments. It will have no meetings which do not naturally conclude with a prayer-meeting and an invitation to penitent sinners to come out and seek the Lord, should any such be present. The Mission exists to save souls, and by saving them and using them to save others.

But Mission people must take holiday sometimes perforce,

and then they look to the Mission to provide them with such holy entertainment as their souls delight in. Services all day long, or, at any rate, during the afternoon, open-air demonstrations, camp meetings, expeditions to other stations, or to mission some new neighbourhood, watch nights, all nights of prayer, are some of the entertainments to which Mission people treat themselves upon extraordinary occasions.

We give two specimens of the sort of employment which fills up unusually large portions of leisure time, and of the results which follow.

One Easter Monday a little band went over from Hastings to New Ramsey, a little town some miles away. The evangelist thus describes how they passed the day :

"In the morning we visited a few families in lodging houses a little out of the town. Some in a little parish called "Hope." Close to the ruins of an old church we saw a man with a wooden leg, accompanied by two children, gathering wood. We spoke to them about their souls, took them to the ruins, and had a prayer meeting then and there. The man found peace. He went home rejoicing, told his wife what had happened and that he intended to lead a new life. In the afternoon we came to his house, found his wife very anxious about her soul. On our knees we brought her to Jesus, and she was made happy. Hallelujah ! Others ventured the same way."

"On Monday, May 10th, we held a camp-meeting here. Friends from Hastings, St. Leonards, Winchelsea, and Rye came to our help. We had a good procession, singing, praying, and short addresses through the principal parts of the town. Crowds of people rushed to their windows and doors, their yards, and lower ends, to hear the singing. When we assembled on the camp ground, the Holy Ghost fell on the speakers, and the Word was with power to many hearts. At the close we formed a ring and five anxious souls came forward, cried for mercy, ventured on Jesus, and five thanked God aloud for having saved them. We afterwards heard of another who found pardon at the same time. The Lord keep them steadfast! The same evening a few friends held a short open-air service on the camp ground, and afterwards went into a cottage close by for a prayer meeting. Four souls found peace, amongst the number a man and his wife about sixty years of age, and the man who lent us the camp ground. To our God be all the glory! "

The following account of the manner in which Good Friday was spent at Barking in 1876, will show what East-enders can do on a holiday or half-holiday, at a very small expense.

" Is it worth while for a large body of mission people to go down to this little town in order to assault the consciences of a few thousand people ? "

Twenty years ago the men of Ilford and Wallend thought it worth their while to march to Barking to fight the fisher-men, and in the drunken frays many a limb was broken. And surely it is worth our while now to go forth in bands to slay the man of sin, and to bind up the broken-hearted. At any rate, so thought a great many soldiers of the Lord on this occasion, and a large number of them have since described the day as the best they ever spent.

Early in the morning the Barking Society met for prayer and they were greatly blessed and helped throughout the day.

At half-past ten a number gathered in time to meet the eleven o'clock train from London, which brought a strong company from Shoreditch, Plaistow, and Soho. These mis-sioned the whole town amidst frequent showers of snow, the cold being so intense as to put the endurance of the sisters to a test which was triumphantly borne for some three hours ; and many a head drooped and many an eye became dim with tears as the burning words of these loving hearts were poured forth.

As the procession was reaching the Hall for a little rest and refreshment, the North Woolwich band came along in their waggon, and the Stoke Newington friends, who had walked half the way, also appeared. In another half hour all were out again, marching through several streets where as yet no stand had been made, on the way to the railway station.

The arrival of large parties from Hackney and Poplar at half-past two made the regiment complete, and marching slowly to the "Horse Pond," an open space in the High Street, a large ring was formed, and here and in the Broadway the experience of one after another was told, until it was time to leave for the indoor meeting at a quarter to seven o'clock.

And glorious experiences they were, coming from men and women of so many grades and employments, from all parts of London, who have been saved by the instrumentality of the Mission from lives of open sin or cold indifference to Christ, and who have been set on fire of love. Many of the roughest men in the town crowded forward with eager interest, and big tears fell while the simple story of salvation sounded out, often from lips more accustomed to cursing and blasphemy.

A tent served for the tea-meeting, at which over two hundred people assembled in relays, leaving always a sufficient number outside to keep up the open-air demonstration.

The meeting held afterwards in the Wesleyan schoolroom was the largest ever gathered by the Mission in Barking. The room, which is said to hold seven or eight hundred people, was packed to the door, and many were pressing around outside, unable to get in. The speaking was in the power of the Holy Ghost, and the impression made was evidently very deep in many cases. One poor woman, with a baby in her arms, fell upon her knees at once to cry for mercy; and some who had frequently scoffed before were evidently so much subdued as to be unable to hold up their heads. The prayer-meeting, however, was spoiled by the necessarily early departure of the London friends, the last train leaving a little after nine.

But in the carriages on the way home the joyful news spread fast, and the Shoreditch company, after singing from Fenchurch Street to the hall in Brick Lane, took one young man who had followed by the hand and led him to Jesus. And how many more are to follow we cannot report ; but of one thing we are sure—all the ends of Barking have heard the salvation of our God.

Easter Monday, 1876, was thus spent by the mission people from two or three of the smaller stations.

Early in the morning a party from Bethnal Green, with violin and concertina, set off for the Finsbury Park gates, where many pleasure seekers wept while the folly and sinfulness of their lives were described, and they were urged to turn to the Lord.

After several hours thus blessedly spent, the company marched singing down to the Abney Park Cemetery gates, where bands from Soho, Stoke Newington and Tottenham falling into the ring, a very large crowd was soon gathered. The power of God fell mightily upon the people, and two stalwart rebels knelt in the midst of the ring to seek mercy. One of these was an old chum of a brother, who formerly joined him in many a drunken spree, but who now gladly pointed him to the Lamb of God, who sets poor drunkards free.

At Whitechapel, the same afternoon, four bands of brethren and sisters were proclaiming the Saviour, 500 sat down to tea, and at the meeting which followed, after a great number had spoken briefly with overpowering effect, six souls sought the Lord.

It may be remarked that in holding such meetings, the object of an holiday, rest and ease, is entirely defeated. But let anyone observe the van-loads of artisans and their wives, who ride out on such days, and frequently on ordinary Mondays, singing and shouting as they journey, racing, jumping, playing skittles, cricket, &c., all the live long day,

H

and returning home at a late hour, too often alas with faculties not merely wearied by healthful exercise, but injured by intoxicating drink. We shall never forget hearing a young man refuse to enter a public-house in the Bethnal Green Road, one Sunday evening, upon the plea that he meant to have "a good spree to-morrow," had no objection to "any amount you like then," but did not wish to spoil the prospect of a day's drinking, by taking too much the evening before !

Mission people often say that Sunday is their "hardest day," and they no doubt return home at the end of the day of rest, and of many a well spent holiday, with their physical power as thoroughly exhausted as though they had been digging foundations, working before the iron furnace, or sewing at sixpence the dozen all day ; but they go to the sweet rest of the Lord's labourers, to recommence their ordinary toil the next morning with increased energy, spirit and joy, and to look forward with a beating heart to the enjoyment of the glorious eternity which they have been helping to secure for others as well as for themselves.

Mission people never like to miss an opportunity to get together, to keep together, to work together, to draw others into their happy circle, where a ceaseless holiday of heavenly merriment drives away the dullness of care, and sorrow, and monotonous toil.

CHAPTER IX.

PROPHETESSES.

" WHAT, women ? "

Yes, women ; and why not, pray ?

" Why, Paul says— "

But stop a bit about Paul. Why did he want to explain how women should be dressed when they prophesied, if he really meant they never should prophesy ? If not allowing them to speak means not permitting their public ministration to the souls of hearers, then how could they prophesy ?

" Oh, but prophesy is a totally different thing to ordinary preaching. A prophetess has a special authority from God."

If the conviction that God authorizes and commands her to speak is sufficient, very good ; that is all we ask. We want nobody, male or female, to do any ordinary preaching. We only wish people to speak when and as they are moved by the Holy Ghost, for only such speaking can break sinners' hearts, and lead them to the Lamb of God. What we maintain is that the Spirit of God does move every converted man and woman, so to speak, in public at times ; and that only by quenching the Spirit and despising prophesyings (of women especially), is the engagement of thousands of women and men in such public testimony prevented.

Poor Paul! We wonder if the dear man knows how his words have been twisted to make him condemn a practice he fostered, no doubt, in every way.

"In Jesus Christ," says he, "there is neither male nor female." He is arguing to show that no human being has any privilege now over another ; that the Gentile may come as near God, do as much for Him, or before Him, as the Jew in every respect, and it is in this connection that he says, "there is neither male nor female."

The greatest care has constantly been taken by many excellent, well-intentioned people, that there should be no females in any prominent place in the Kingdom of Christ, but the males are everywhere. Paul says—God says :

"There is neither male nor female."

Now that is a grand principle, clear as noon-day, and which anybody can act upon with ease. There is to be no distinction between any two people now on account of any merely casual circumstance. The Roman, the Englishman, has as much right to preach the Gospel, to exercise any sacred authority or power, as the Jew ; and the female has as much right to preach the Gospel, to exercise any sacred office, as the male.

Why ? What is the foundation of this grand principle ? Nothing short of the great truth—" Ye are all one in Christ Jesus." It makes no matter how anybody is born now. Male or female, they must be born again of the Spirit, or die for ever. It makes no matter to what family or sex any one belongs now. They must not attempt to be God's priests unless they are made "priests unto God" by the Holy Ghost. And every converted person, male or female, is so honoured, for He "hath made *us*." It makes no matter how anyone may be regarded by men now, honoured, ordained, called out, stationed, commended, testimonialized, titled, diplomaed, or what not, they must not preach unless they are filled with the Spirit of the Lord. It makes no matter how anyone may be disregarded either, scorned, repelled, refused, insulted, decried, written against, misrepresented, slandered, they must confess Christ *before men* (no matter who says they should only do it before women), or He will not confess them before His Father and the holy angels.

We can conceive of no escape from this clear principle, and the all-comprehending truth upon which it is built. If God would only have saved the two sexes in two different ways, or damned them, if unbelieving or disobedient, to two separate hells, then this monstrous distinction between men and women's rights in connection with the preaching of the Gospel might have had some show of reason.

But God utterly repudiates any dividing line whatever, and therefore, depend upon it, unless the female servants of the Lord bestir themselves, quit themselves like men of God, and be strong for Him, He will not give them the lot of the men of God in Heaven. Paul, who expressed this great principle of absolute equality before God so often, never in his life so outrageously set it aside as to oppose the preaching of any woman.

Will anybody explain to us what course Paul took when he and his friends stayed at the house of Philip, the evangelist, who had four virgin daughters prophetesses ? Four in one family ! Four ! Talk about the little extravagances of The Christian Mission ! Four in one family !

Whatever had Philip the evangelist been about ? He used to be a man full of the Holy Ghost, guided as by an unseen hand in every step and word. Perhaps it was while he was away serving tables, or on an evangelistic tour, that his four daughters broke out with this prophesying unbeknown to him. But was Mrs. Philip dead ? Whatever did mamma say ? And what did papa say when he got home ? Why did he not at least stop them before this dreadful Paul came along, who did not " suffer a woman to speak ? " Was he not afraid Paul would report him and his daughters to "the elders at Jerusalem," and "have the whole thing put a stop to," or Phillip discharged from being a deacon?

How could Paul endure living in the house with four female preachers, if he had been persecuting their sisters in every city? Whichever way he turned, the reproachful glance of a female preacher must have fallen upon him (and that is no "light affliction," even if it be "but for a moment"). Surely he hurried off as soon as possible without giving them the chance of beginning to exercise their gifts against him! He seemed to be in a hurry, too, when he came; for he had only spent a day with the *brethren* at Ptolemais. But when he got to the house where the four female preachers lived, he "tarried many days." No doubt, he found, as many a one has since, that preaching does not prevent a good woman from looking well to the affairs of her house. We know that many a working-man's house whose wife is a Christian Mission speaker will bear comparison with any home supported on the same income.

It is perfectly clear that Paul and the four female preachers got on admirably together; so much so that, when Agabus came down and told them what awaited Paul at Jerusalem, the dear girls cried like to break *his* heart, which was a very stout one, to say nothing of their own, and would fain have kept him for any length of time rather than that he should come to any harm.

Now upon Paul's arrival at Jerusalem he gathered the elders together and " declared *particularly* what things God had wrought amongst the Gentiles by his ministry." Surely the lively recollection of those four young female preachers at Cæsarea led him to particularize how completely God had stopped the mouths of the female speakers by his ministry even as He stopped the mouths of the lions in Daniel's time. Surely he said a little word about the great disorder in the church at Cæsarea, and made a little suggestion or two? But there is no trace of anything of the sort, and if those dear cautious old gentlemen did not send a letter to all the females to "abstain from public speaking," we may be quite certain neither Paul nor any one of them thought it a "necessary thing" for there to be any such abstention. Oh, that every elder to-day were equally wise !

Does any one charge us with trifling with a solemn theme ? We are in no mood for trifling. We have reasonable hopes of being in a short time with Paul and all his female preachers, for scores and hundreds we doubt not he raised up, if not many thousands, and oh, if we can say anything to clear our brother's memory, in any mind, of this absurd calumny, we shall feel it a double pleasure to meet him in the "morning." Oh, if we can, even by a little playfulness, stir the thoughts of many and arouse the female members of God's Church (always the bitterest opponents of woman's preaching mission) to enquire, and especially to enquire *of the Lord* direct in prayer, as to their duty in this respect, we shall have well spent the time. For Satan has indeed well managed to prevent the more attractive sex from proclaiming Christ.

What *is* woman's work if not to preach ? The devil made her his first preacher on earth, and the result of her first sermon was the ruin of us all. And now she must not preach any more ! Of course not. Devil !—how clever a deceiver you are !

Woman's first wrong step was looking too much after food, and too little after divine things, and the devil and the churches he has so largely mastered would fain point woman in the same direction still. "Cook! cook! cook! Oh, noble woman, behold the object of thy existence !"

One of the first fruits of woman's sin was that she had to put on an "apron." The devil and the churches detest to see her without one. Pretty, silk, ornamented, tasteful, useless if you like ; but woman you must stick to the apron ! If you want to be particularly pious or great you may wear a long white one with red-crossed armlets in the Hospital, and we will saint you and medal you for it; but above the apron you never must aspire, woman!

Your sire fell, it is true, as well as you; but then he can rise again; in Christ were all (men of course) made alive. Men often begin under an apron and finish in a villa; but you, woman, the apron, always the apron! In the villa, if possible in the mansion, aye, even in the palace if you can; but remember never fail to wear the apron. And fastening your children to its strings lead them to look upon it as the necessary, one, only vocation of a woman.

But stay! The double-faced devil will consent to thy advancement to the most public position possible if it be but to lead souls to hell. The stage! Oh, yes, by all means, go on to the stage. Dance there half-dressed, if you like. Take part unblushingly in the representation of the vilest iniquity before a dense crowd of the highest and most learned in the land. Sing, speak, perform, be shameless, be a great, public, constant lie, and you shall be worshipped by whole nations for it all. Nobles shall pour their wealth at your feet for the honour of your hand. The greatest monarchs of the earth shall bow to you, the whole press of every Christian people shall belaud you. The "religious papers" reserve a little quiet column on purpose for such names as yours! Every kingdom of the world shall be yours if you like to take the foremost part in leading men down to the pit.

But to stand upon that very same stage to lead men to Heaven! To speak, or sing, or pray there! Oh, horrible! Abomination! Degradation of your sex! Disgrace to religion! Outrage upon society! Society!—the very society that would gloat over your performances as an actress, and shut you out of its circles because you were one!

And as to appearing in the open air, at the street-corners, addressing men, braving insult, and standing amidst the godless multitudes to speak aloud for God,—why, you must be demented—lost to every sense of propriety, utterly without respect for yourself, to dream of anything of the sort!

Surely, you will not make such an exhibition of yourself, and disgrace family and friends for ever ?

Woman of God, make thy choice ! There is the stage—there is the open-air stand. The multitudes will crowd to hear thee—no matter what thy name, thy position, thy abilities—simply because thou art a woman. If thou, by the power of God, no matter whether with finished oratory, or with faltering, disconnected phrases, shalt move their hearts, they will come, and come again, and thou wilt see many of them fall at the feet of thy Jesus, if thou wilt but go forth and speak to them. Thy God says to thee as much as to anyone, "Go ye into all the world, and preach the Gospel to every creature." There is neither "male nor female" in the eye of thy Creator, thy King, thy Saviour, thy Judge. Wilt thou obey Him ? It may cost thee all thy friends, thy reputation, thy comfort in life, thy home, thy fortune, thy health, thy life, thy all ; but " He freely gave Himself up for us all "—for women as well as for men. Wilt thou give up all for him ? Wilt thou hear the Master's voice, and gladly answer, when He calleth, " Here am I—send me, send me." Oh, woman, Heaven, and earth, and Hell are eager to catch thy answer ! Wilt thou ?

How many " careless women " there are in Israel still who "do not (will not) see their obligation to do so ; " who " do not feel qualified for such a work " (how can anyone until they have attempted in the power of God, the one great qualification, to undertake it) ; who " do not feel prepared for such sacrifices," as God felt prepared before the foundation of the world, to make for them ; who " dare not, cannot (that is, will not) take such a step." "Their system could not endure such a strain ! " How will their system endure the Judgment Day, when they see millions of damned souls who might have been sheep, had there been more shepherdesses—had woman had her proper place in God's kingdom ?

Oh ! should the hearts that are most tender turn away from a dying world because it is not thought proper to save them in

God's appointed way by preaching ?   Oh ! should the gentle, loving voices, that first spoke of Jesus to all these multitudes in their early days, be silent while, in maturer years, they rush down to perdition ?   Oh ! should those whose mission it is confessedly to minister to the ease, the rest, the comfort of man look after the *animal*, and leave the soul to be ministered to by men—or by nobody, if men's ministrations are not listened to ?   God forbid !   He does forbid !   " Let not man prevail ! "   " We ought to obey God rather than men !"

" But women are not qualified for the management of spiritual, still less of business, affairs ! "

Indeed ! are they not ?   How many huge mansions and large families are under the care of a woman, and well cared for ?   How many millions of money are gained, and how many millions of souls drowned in drink yearly in public-houses and hotels, under a landlady ?

We do not argue for the employment of anyone in any task they are not fully qualified for ; but we insist that disqualification must be proved—not merely asserted—in every case, and that a woman who is duly qualified to manage shall be allowed to do so.   You need not protect, or support, or counsel such a woman much !   She will manage everybody, and overcome everything, if you but just give her the position—the opportunity !   Leave the rest to God and her. And oh ! take care with your proprieties and your talk about " Paul," lest you should be found to fight against God.

Not allow a woman to usurp authority over a man !   Ye married men, what are the *facts?*   Aye, and ye moon-struck youths too ?   Is it not the very joy of your life to submit in everything from the choice of a business—a town—a horse to that of a stud, or a salt-cellar to the sweet little gentle influence that can usurp to any extent, before you know it has done so ?

Does not Paul (that sole authority you know upon these things) let out the whole truth, and nothing but the truth, when he says, that " a married man leaves caring for God,"

and sets himself to please his wife ! Thank God, you will allow
exceptions to Paul's doctrine here. Job was one, and
Abraham was one, and Moses was one. But did not the wife
of each of these heroes have much to do with all their affairs ?
Did they never usurp at all ? Ask the sons of Ishmael !

What nonsense it all is ! Why cannot people leave God
alone to manage, and to set up whom he pleases ? Did He
not make a woman a judge in Israel, and has He not the
eternal right to make as many more female judges as the
necessities of Israel may demand ?

Is it not time somebody usurped authority over all the
millions of professedly Christian men, who stand idle while
the world is perishing ! If a house were burning, and a
woman finding all the firemen gaping below usurped
authority and showed how to save it, would the Insurance
Companies object ?

Did anybody cry shame, when the captain of a brig having
fallen ill on the Atlantic, a few years since, his wife usurped
his authority and brought the vessel into port ?

The helm of many a church is in feeble enough hands to-
day ! Members idling, chatting, entertaining one another
and their dear pastor, while the souls around are perishing
for lack of the knowledge that churches should diffuse ! May
God raise up some spiritual Grace Darlings, who, even if
they have to row alone in the boat they manage, may bring
salvation to thousands who through the mismanagement and
carelessness and stupidity of men, are ready to perish !
Grace Darlings, wherever you are, for ye are legion, come forward in spite of earth and hell, and usurp authority to save !

If the Christian Mission ceased to exist to-day, it would
have amply justified its past career, and covered its originator with glory, if only because it has brought forward
again to the light that chosen instrumentality of the kingdom of heaven, Female Ministry, and allowed of the demonstration of its utility and Power—its divine right.

The Christian Mission woman, at a street corner, can get

and hold as large a crowd by even giving out a hymn, as the most eloquent of its male evangelists. The power of the woman's speaking, as her own heart melts and her tears flow at the sight of the lost around her, streams of tears from eyes that never wept for sin before, heaving breasts and broken hearts attest it, a million times, every Sabbath day!

The Christian Mission preacher on the platform as she teaches the wondering audiences, who crowd to hear the things concerning Jesus Christ, finds ample reply to every hostile criticism in the mighty working with her of God's Holy Spirit, and as she leads score after score of penitents to the Saviour's feet, catches in His smile something to light up the path His followers would make so thorny and so dark.

May the Christian Mission long perpetuate such marvels, till they cease by their multiplicity to be marvellous!

But your female ministers get married! Well, and quite right too! God bless them and their children, if they have any! He has already blessed every husband beyond measure, who secures such a prize.

But then they stop preaching! Indeed! Do they? The most constant female preachers we know are married women! No woman deserves a good husband and a nice home so much as a female preacher, and even supposing that they so far lose their religion, when they marry, as to cease to preach, or suppose that household care and ill-health prevent their doing so, what worse are they than the millions of women of Israel, who never began to do their duty? Is not the work of their past, the memory of their faithfulness, the salvation of the souls they led to Christ, as precious, if not apparently more so, when they turn aside to folly—to the unspeakably awful folly of an extinguished lamp?

"The Bridegroom cometh!" Women of God, disregarding every other voice, "Go ye *forth* to meet Him!" Let His path be illuminated by the gleam of your light, which was no more given to be hid "under a bed" or "a bushel," active, or passive private life, than that of your brethren.

CHAPTER X.

THE SAINTS IN HOSPITAL.

AFTER leaving the gin-palace behind them, the only palaces in which Christian Mission people ever rest are the Palaces of Pain, which stand here and there in the metropolis and in every large town, with ward after ward thronged with the suffering poor, bearing all manner of sickness and disease, or awaiting the result of accident.

The advent of a mission man into such a place is generally quite an event in the eyes of many other inhabitants of the palace beside the patient himself. There can be no sort or degree of suffering to which doctors and nurses, and even patients who are long there, do not grow quite accustomed; but to see somebody to whom pain is pleasure, and death is victory—somebody who is quite as anxious about the souls of doctors and nurses, and fellow-patients and visitors as they can be about his body—this is certainly a phenomenon, " a very peculiar and interesting case."

Here is a man from the dockyard. A mass of iron has fallen upon the lower half of his body, and he is all but dead when they arrive with him at the hospital.

The doctor comes and looks very serious, for it is an almost hopeless case; but as he proceeds, with all possible speed, to sew up the lacerated body, " This is glorious!" cries the patient.

"What is glorious?" asks the doubting doctor, "this pain?"

"No, doctor; that is not glorious, but Jesus is. He makes me feel so happy in the midst of it."

Says the doctor to the evangelist, a few minutes later—

"He would have died under the operation if he had not been mad with religion."

His friends find the poor man, though unable to move his body, waving his hand and shouting the praises of God.

"Oh," says he, "I thought I should have been in heaven before now; but oh, I am so happy!"

"Do not weep, my dear," he adds to his sad wife, "I am ready for heaven."

The convalescent patients naturally gather round his bed to hear the marvellously joyous testimonies he loves to give, and which his whole demeanour so admirably bears out, to the blessedness and power of the love of Christ.

Thank God! he came out again, however, contrary to the expectation of everyone, weakened and injured for life, but happy in the Lord, and ready for suffering and poverty as well as for heaven.

About eight o'clock one evening, a poor man is brought to the Poplar Hospital in a cart, wherein he has been jolted over four miles of heavy road from the Millwall Dock. He had been helping some mates to clear away their tools from a vessel's deck after work was done, when a spar had fallen upon him and so crushed his body that no skill could prolong his life.

But as soon as they have laid him upon his bed in the accident ward, and allowed his wife and children to gather around him, he says:

"Look to Jesus. I've no condemnation. It's all right; you must live to the Lord."

They leave him in a couple of hours, hoping to see him again in the morning. But shortly after they are gone a nurse observes a great change for the worse, and asks:

"Do you know Jesus?"

"*Know* Him ? *Know* Him ? " he replies.

> "He is my Prophet, Priest and King,
> Who did for me Salvation bring,
> And while I've breath, I mean to sing,
> Christ for me.' "

He used to sing these words very often in the Limehouse Hall, clapping the hymn-book with his hand for joy.

"Are you afraid to die ? " the nurse asks.

"I'm not afraid to die. All is well," he answers, and praying as long as his breath holds out, "God bless my dear wife," he flies away from the land of broken bones and hospitals to the land beyond the river.

Early one morning a poor man is borne to the London Hospital whose body has been so dreadfully torn by machinery that life cannot possibly last twenty-four hours. His spine dislocated, mortification set in, pain has already ceased when they lay him on the bed, and it is only for him now to lie there and die.

When friends come, he assures them that "all is well," begs them to pray, joining heartily in every petition.

After awhile he becomes much agitated with regard to the salvation of his father and mother and the other members of his family, who are "out of the way." But as to himself there is no trouble.

"Oh," says he, "the blood ! the blood ! the blood ! It cleanseth me from all sin ! It does, it does, it does !

> 'My Jesus to know and to feel his blood flow
> 'Tis life everlasting—'Tis heaven below.' "

He is incessantly speaking, praying, or singing of or to Jesus. "Thy will be done ! thy will be done ! thy will be done ! " he cries.

A last hour of intense agony, and at three o'clock another happy sufferer is fled away to everlasting repose.

Sometimes, however, Mission people go to the hospital for long terms of trial, under which, however, the Lord does not allow their patience, their fortitude, or their cheeriness to diminish in the least.

Here lies a young man dying of consumption.

"Never mind," says he to a visitor one day ; "I shall be in heaven soon. I shall never be with you at class again ; but tell them, 'We shall gather at the river.'" Told of some of the dying words of a former Mission associate, he exclaims, "Bless God! I shall see him soon."

Another day he detains a friend two hours telling him how easy it is to die in the arms of Jesus. The nurse brings tea, into which he puts some sugar of his own. Both sugar and spoons are beyond the hospital supplies, and his friend remarks, "That's no good ; we have nothing to stir it with."

"Bless you," he merrily replies, "that's like religion— sometimes bad to take ; but we get the best last."

He sings, "My Jesus, I love thee ; I know thou art mine ! "

Putting one hand upon his breast, and pointing with the other upwards, he says, "Bless God! I shall soon be there;" and then sings again—

> "No chilling winds, no poisonous breath
> Can reach that healthful shore ;
> Sickness and sorrow, pain and death
> Are felt and feared no more."

Standing by such bedsides, we must confess that this verse, and many, many more, are thrown into strange confusion in the mind. Is it, after all, only on the other side of the river that "sickness and sorrow, pain and death, are felt and feared no more ?" How can we fear sickness and sorrow, pain and death, which seem only to bring so many extra loads of light and joy and heavenly glory down amongst the sin-stricken children of men ? When asked to visit somebody who is ill, and especially somebody " in the hospital," there is a pang that no friendly heart can help feeling, a sorrow for the suffering, and a sort of half-dread of witnessing their pain, and of losing them as the result of it. But when one gets to the bedside, where is the pain? Where is the sorrow? Where is the gloom? There seems to be nothing but a little heaven below, and one comes away hardly able to realise that anything serious is the matter, much less that a friend is going perhaps to pass away. There is a strange struggle between sorrow and joy, an odd feeling of shame for having expected to see anything sad, and at the same time for not feeling sadder. And by the time one has got through the long corridors and down the broad staircases and out into the busy street, one can only feel disposed to hurry along for Jesus, sure that "nothing shall harm you if you be followers of that which is good."

Here lies a converted infidel, poor old man, labouring for breath, and yet as happy as anyone can possibly be.

"Oh," says he, "it's all so bright—so bright! It seems to me as though I was looking through a lovely valley, and everything is so beautiful that I can't describe it to you. Ten thousand suns shining in their strength would be as nothing to the brightness of my prospect. The doctors have given me up, and I may die to-night; but you never need be in any doubt where Cooper's gone—glory, glory!"

A visitor one day asked him about his present view of the truth of the Gospel.

"It is all real—it is all real," he replied, with the greatest energy he could command.

Asked to visit a sister who has been lying there for months and is now thought likely to die, we enter the long ward just in the twilight of a summer's evening, and are unable to recognize the swollen face until a hand is stretched out and a gasped word of welcome reaches us.

"Well, how are you?"

"Oh, happy praise the Lord! My throat is very bad, but I can bear it."

"I hope you will get better, after all."

I

" I don't mind a bit, either way. I am perfectly content with my Father's will."

" It is you that used to visit the public-houses with tracts, isn't it ?"

" Yes ; and I did it for the Lord, and I know I shall meet some of the poor people in heaven."

After a little more communion with one another we join in prayer, just as happily as if we were out in some open-air stand in perfect health ; and her hearty " Amen " and " Praise the Lord," whispered though they be through her almost closed throat, make the little prayer-meeting much more lively than many a larger one that could be discovered amongst the healthy.

Two sisters employed about the hospital, who have been brought to the Lord at our Hall hard by, come to inquire how she is.

" Oh, nicely, bless you ! I am so glad to see the young starting in the way, for there is so much to be done."

A German baker lies in an even more dangerous state ; but the terrible pain of body he bears so patiently does not prevent his being filled with anxiety for the poor sinner on the next bed, dying without God and without hope. " Do just pray vit dat man a leetle ; he is not saved—he be dying without my Savior." And we learned that, true to his mission in the world—in the hospital—he had succeeded in getting the dying man at his side to cry, " God be merciful to me, a sinner ! " ere it was for ever too late.

"And now, Brother D., I must go ; what about yourself ?"

" Oh, I be saved to de fullest ; I have Shesus vit me to the end ! "

" And how do you feel about leaving your wife and little one ? "

" Oh, sir ! " and the poor, worn face lighted up with the joy of confident faith ; " Shesus' friends vill be their friends."

And so they have.

The instance just recorded is by no means the only one

recently brought to our notice in which the salvation of a wretched dying soul has been brought about in the hospital.

A man who had very often stood and listened at the noon-day service held in front of the Whitechapel Hall, met with an accident, and was carried in a dying state to the London Hospital. He sent at once for somebody from the Hall. Our gipsy evangelist immediately went to see him. As he was known to be dying, perfect liberty was accorded to both, and soon the poor sinner and this young soul-saver were locked in each others arms, while both cried to God for the pardon of the sinking soul. In a few minutes tears of anguish were exchanged for tears of joy, and the dying man could calmly lie down to rest for ever.

A poor woman, covered and blinded with smallpox in its most awful form—for the time being, a leper as white as snow, exhaling death to all around, but breathing the atmosphere of Heaven none the less.

The doctor and nurses had told her it was quite uncertain whether she would live a few hours or a day or two.

"It's a blessed thing to be quite certain about the end, whenever it may come, Mary," said her visitor.

"Yes, bless the Lord!—bless the Lord! Praise God!—praise God!"

Articulation was very difficult, her mouth being swollen and ulcerated, and she seemed to be able to think or say little more than this, which she continually repeated—"Bless the Lord! Praise God!" She had not a living relation in the world to her knowledge, and her life had been filled with the most painful trials. No wonder she beat time with her poor, swollen hand, though unable to join in singing—

> "Light in the darkness, sailor,
>   Day is at hand ;
> See o'er the foaming billows
>   Fair Haven's land.

> Drear was the voyage, sailor,
>   Now almost o'er,
> Watch the bright and morning star, and
>   Pull for the shore.
>
> Pull for the shore, sailor, pull for the shore ;
> Heed not the rolling wave, but bend to the oar ;
> Drear was the voyage, sailor, now almost o'er,
> Leave the poor old stranded wreck, and pull for the shore."

She was off to the Happy Land at half-past four in the morning, long before we were up. " Bless the Lord !— praise God ! "

CHAPTER XI.

WHY WE SUCCEED.

THE Mission has been a great success, of course, simply because God has made and led and sustained it. But we will endeavour to explain more fully the causes which have contributed to this.

I. The Mission succeeds by aiming at immediate results.

We have always *aimed* at immediate and definite results, believing that the Gospel of Christ, properly preached in the demonstration of the Spirit, and with power, ought to prove, must prove, *visibly* as well as in the heart, its Divine efficiency. What, indeed, can be the use of preaching, unless it secures some *immediate* result ? Especially must this question arise when the audience largely consists of those who are little disposed even to listen to the Gospel : who have never come under its sound before, and never may again.

Here is a man who has not "been into church or chapel, except to be married," since he can remember. Next him sits one who says, "Me pray ? I never did such a thing in my life ! I do not know what to say." They are usually together in the public-house on a Sunday evening, or strolling along the streets. There is not a soul amongst all their acquaintance who has any more regard for God than they have themselves. It seems incredible, indeed, that those two men should be so completely enlightened, convinced, persuaded, overcome, and spiritually transformed in a service of two or three hours' duration, that all old things shall pass away, and all things become new. Only faith in God could render such a miracle conceivable or possible.

But, after all, is it not far harder to conceive of a change so radical being accomplished at all, if it be not done *now at once?* Every influence which surrounds these men is calculated to prevent their coming again. If the truth takes little or no hold of them, what is likely to induce them to return? If the truth does take sufficient hold of their consciences to make them feel very uncomfortable about their awful state, and they nevertheless go. away undecided, are they likely to come and subject themselves again to the torture? All this supposing even that they remain in life and in the same neighbourhood still. But we are dealing with dying men, and with men whom work and a thousand other circumstances may cause to migrate any day.

A sailor heard us in the open-air one night. "God seemed to speak in my heart and tell me I was all wrong," he told us afterwards.

He leaned over to one of the speakers there, and said, "Where do you go to? I should like to come sometime."

"It is in K—— Street," was the reply. "*Come to-night. Whatever you do, come to-night.*"

He came, after going home for a wash, and sat very uneasily while three brief, simple addresses were delivered by working people on the salvation they had received. At the end of the speaking, while the hymn was sung beginning—

> "Come to the Saviour, come to the Saviour,
> Thou sin-stricken offspring of man."

little persuasion was needed to induce him to step out before all the people and kneel down before God. "I don't know what to say," he said. Poor fellow! he had been far more familiar with the Lord's name in oaths and curses than in any other way hitherto. But his child-like confession of sin, and of his determination to give it all up if the Lord would only forgive him, was soon made, and the mighty comfort of the Holy Ghost poured into his happy soul. He voluntarily signed the pledge at once, and went away to sea in a few days rejoicing in God. We may never see him on earth again. What prospect should we have of meeting him in heaven if he had not been turned *at once* on that decisive night from darkness unto light, and from the power of Satan unto God ?

It may naturally enough be said, " Oh, but how can you rely upon the permanence of a work so suddenly begun and ended ? " We simply reply, " Take the worst view of the case. Take it that these people relapse into sin. Is it any worse result than would have followed from leaving them to delay even a professed decision ?."

" But may not sinners be led to deceive themselves into the founding of a false hope upon a sudden and temporary emotion ? "

Undoubtedly there are such cases ; but in dealing with the class to which we preach there is little risk of such a delusion lasting many hours. Amongst those who have all their lives paid formal service to God, who are surrounded daily by regular attendants upon Divine worship, and whose characters and habits have already been outwardly conformed in a very considerable degree to the law of God, self-deception may exist for years. Such persons may have sat in a certain place, or even been members of the church for a long period, without having ever truly repented, or sought and found the forgiveness of their sins. They may be induced, under some sympathetic feeling, or some able oratory, to believe that, because Jesus died for them, they live in Him, although they have never been born again, and are conscious of no real change in themselves, and the delusion may be kept up with the singing of hymns and the saying of prayers, and the study of Scripture, and by labours in God's vineyard for years, yea, for a lifetime, unchecked.

But not so with working people. The universal consciousness of right and wrong makes it perfectly clear to the
rudest minds that to become one of the Lord's people is to
enter upon a' new life. The young convert must go home
to ask God's blessing upon his food, and to kneel down and
pray, in a household where such things have never been
done before, and where they must produce general amusement, if not stronger opposition. He must take no further
part in the songs he sang up to that evening, and must sing
words that shock his friends as much as a lewd music hall
ditty would shock polite ears. He must keep clear of the
oaths, and curses, and obscenities which have, perhaps, been
flowing from his lips like a torrent hitherto, and must not so
much as stand by to listen to the vile conversation which,
even if "a quiet man" himself, he has had daily to hear from
others. He must keep outside the public-houses and places
of amusement which have been his constant resort, for,
whatever may be the idea of other people, it is a universally
received maxim with the working classes that any one who
is religious has no business in such places or among such
company. But conformity to an imperfect extent with
even a part of this new programme must render him the
object of general remark, inquiry, and ridicule.

"When I went to my workshop the first morning, I knew
I should have them all on to me," said one. "So I was
determined to let them see at once I didn't care for them.
I just laid my little hymn-book down upon the bench in
front of me, and sang away while I worked. They couldn't
make it out, and said I shouldn't keep on long like that.
Some gave me three weeks, and some gave me till Christmas
time came round ; but, thank God, I am at it still, and my
work seems to be far easier to get through than ever it did
before."

And then, not content with this, the Mission at once
comes down upon them with a request to come to the open-
air service the very day after their conversion, and they

are closely questioned as to the reason, if they fail to be there.

" I was very sorry," voluntarily explained one, the evening after his conversion at the in-door meeting, "I was very sorry that I could not get to you in time this evening. I had to be in the Strand all day, and it kept me late."

The most solemn warnings, as to the half-hearted and those who fail to confess the Master before men, are dealt out without sparing to all our people, and thus no one can be with us for two days without being given clearly to understand that there must be a radical change in every part of his life, if he is to enter heaven at last.

Sometimes a man says, with blushing averted face, " I am afraid I shall not be able to get with you much, for my wife is sick " (of religion), or " I have to work so late," or " to get up so early," or " I live so far away." " Yes, I will come on Sunday, if I can." But he won't. Either he was not truly converted, or the first few hours battling have been too much for his faith. He has gone back to the beggarly elements of the world. " I will come to-morrow night. The reason I stopped was the doctor ordered me some stout." Poor man ! Broken pledge, broken faith, broken connection, broken hope ! By-and-bye, if he does not come back and go all lengths for God, broken heart, and soul wounded and sore broken for ever !

We are far from denying the possibility of mistake, self deception or even hypocrisy, notwithstanding all this. But we think it will be evident enough to every thoughtful mind, that anything of the sort is to the last degree improbable, if not all but impossible. Have we not almost realized as fully as was ever done before, the glorious description of the early Church, " Of the rest *durst* no man join himself unto them ? "

We attribute the success of the Mission mainly to the fact that it has never aimed at anything short of the full and glorious apostolic programme of saving people in a moment "from this untoward generation," and that those who have laboured in it, have always done so in unwavering confidence, that the power of the Holy Ghost was sufficient to accomplish this miraculous effect in a moment in the heart of the very vilest sinner. The Mission is one huge living testimony to the power of Christ to save to the uttermost all that come unto God by Him—to save instantly—to convert —to create anew—to make clean. All hail the power of Jesu's name! Alleluiah!

Does anybody say, "But these people do not stand. You do not always find the work genuine." Alas, alas, this is only too true, and only those who are familiar with the fearful risks to which these people are exposed, can realize the miracle of the preservation of so many. But while the wanderings of some make up bitter sorrows for us, thank God we cannot be discouraged while these very losses exhibit to us in all the more striking prominence the mighty work wrought, and daily being perfected in so many as do stand. We know only too well how far short we come of the success we would desire; but all the more for that we bless God daily for what we see and hear of his wonderful works.

Shall we stop here? Why not add one other word about this question of standing? "Let him," saith the Lord, "that thinketh he standeth, take heed lest he fall."

The well-brought-up respectable man, who has always attended a place of worship and maintained an outward show of respect for religion, may, after his conversion, sink down into the very carelessness and worldliness which distinguished him before without remark, except it be on the part of a faithful pastor, or an intimate spiritual friend. Will it be found at last, after all, that the proportion of backsliders was smaller amidst the cushions and rolls of the churches, than amidst the lists of mission agencies? We doubt it.

We do our uttermost to secure thorough work in the first instance. We warn every man to an extent which many of our friends think excessive; but which we look upon as absolutely essential, to beware lest he receive the grace of God in vain, lest turning from his righteousness he commit iniquity and die therein, lest after having preached to others he himself become a cast-away, lest having "escaped the pollutions of the world, through the knowledge of the Lord and Saviour Jesus Christ," he should be " again entangled therein and overcome." Thank God for the multitudes who remain steadfast, immovable, always abounding in the work of the Lord ! But we count it no reproach to the work any more than to our Master, to admit that many at some point or other, perhaps the very first day the call to sacrifice comes, turn away and follow no more after him.

II. The Mission succeeds by making the most of the converts.

When people are *converted,* as in the Apostles' days, so now, they not only love and bless God, but it is easy for those who have given them a hand, and lifted them on to their feet, to lead them about the city anywhere—marching, singing, praising and blessing God, where "all the people " can see them. The people always did, and always will run together wondering at such a sight. Upon this principle of utilizing every convert to proclaim the glad tidings to others, the Mission has always diligently acted, and therefore at every station it has opened, a band of men and women have been organized and trained daily to attack the kingdom of the wicked one, and daily to expect to gain recruits for the ranks.

Everybody can stand by and show themselves on the Lord's side—nearly everyone can help to sing, and there are very few people, if any, who cannot if they will, say a few simple words for Jesus, for out of the abundance of the heart the mouth speaketh, and if the mouth speaketh not, it is, with very rare exceptions indeed, for want of sufficient abundance in the heart.

" But do you let young converts speak at once ? "

To be sure. We urge them to do so. Why not ?

" May it not do them harm, and bring a great reproach upon the cause if they go back ? "

Undoubtedly it may.   But there is little risk of getting
people to speak for Jesus too early in public, as any one will
find who tries, and a very great risk indeed of people
settling down to think they really cannot if they don't begin
at once. Therefore we like to get them over the bar in the full
tide of their first love, and their future efficiency is comparatively easy.   As to the reproach of the cause, what of
that ?   Has not God in the Scriptures put before the whole
world and the devil, as prominently as any other facts, the
faults and backslidings of His own people ?

Has He not given universal publicity to the fact that the
General Superintendent of the Egyptian Mission was shut
out of the promised land for losing his temper one day at
his faithless, grumbling followers, who were all in a body
condemned as unworthy of the grand inheritance promised
to their fathers ?

Has He not made known to the whole world that one of
Jesus Christ's most trusted friends and associates—his
cashier, in fact, was a downright swindler ?

Has He not assured us that the great Apostle who first
proclaimed the gospel to a dying world tried to play Mr.
Facing-two-ways, and had to be publicly exposed for it by
another great Apostle ?

Oh, yes ! A poor little weakly kingdom may well tremble
in every limb, and fear every despatch and speech may
bring about some ruinous result, but the Kingdom of God
is strong enough to step out boldly and to bear any amount
of disgrace and reproach, so overwhelming is the cloud of
glory that perpetually hangs over it, and so irresistible the
almighty force by which it is propelled.

" But may not harm be done by ignorant persons attempt-
ing to explain the mysteries of religion ?"

Certainly, and we never wish anybody to do that in the
Mission. We simply ask people to speak what they do know
and testify to that they have seen, and the mere fact of their
having become so totally changed as to stand there at all,

speaks with a voice that completely stills in every honest mind cavilling about their words, their manners, and their defects.

Suppose you were to try to persuade a mother to keep her baby from babbling to the dishonour of the family intelligence and education !

" But babies are kept in the nursery and not allowed to babble before everybody.".

Just so, and the Mission professes to be God's nursery, and after having most imprudently and improperly, if you like, allowed its babies' voices to be heard even in the most public streets, has arrived at this result that it has now got *hundreds* of men and women who can make it clear to every passer-by that a great change has passed upon them which God has wrought, and that He is able and willing to do as much for whosoever shall call upon His name. And besides these the Mission has hosts of babies just learning to prattle who will swell the numbers of regular speakers soon.

" What, women too speaking in public. Is that right ? "

Yes it is, as we have already endeavoured to show in our chapter on Prophetesses.

" But are such men and women qualified to teach the great truths of religion ?" Surely the answer must come from experience and not from theory. If such men so speak as to get a hearing; if they so speak as to convey to the minds and hearts of others the facts about sin and salvation, so vital for all to receive ; if they so speak that many believe to the saving of their souls, upon what grounds shall they be condemned ?

True they may murder the Queen's English, making it quite unnecessary to assure their hearers—

" I am no scholard, my dear friends. You must just take it rough as it comes from my heart."

But if the hearers' grammar is on a par with the speaker's, and if they do take it as it comes, what then ?

They may not be apt at quoting Scripture ; but if they

convey the great truths of revelation in homely words to the heart, do they not really carry out the purpose of the Bible as fully as if they used its language?

They may not be great logicians; but if they confound both small and great with the overwhelming argument, "I haven't been to no college, friends, and I can't say much to yer; but I know one thing—God has forgiven my sins, and He'll forgive yours and all, if you let him," is it not enough?

They may not have studied rhetoric; but if moved by the Holy Ghost, and, speaking with all the energy of quenchless love, they leave upon every heart the deep conviction that they are in earnest, and that they are right, is not their eloquence sufficient?

But surely the time has passed for us to plead for the ministry of working men to their own class. How great and wide-spread an effect the oratory of earnest, ignorant men can produce, has been abundantly proved in many national matters within the last twenty years.

One evening, as an open-air service was just commencing, a dear brother, on his way home from work, came by. He was induced to stop for half-an-hour, and when he stood forward, with his hands and face begrimed with his daily toil, and with his slop and top-boots, all muddy as they were, a large and attentive congregation of working people was at once assured. Nobody could think he was "paid for it." When a miserable scoffer would fain have interrupted him, a sturdy navvy cried out, "Let him alone. It's all right what he says. I work with him every day. Go on, my boy."

The likeliest of all people to carry on successful work for the salvation of the masses must necessarily be those who have themselves been brought to Christ by such efforts.

"I bless God that ever this Mission came here," said a man, the other day; "I lived here twenty years, and nobody ever asked me if I had a soul, until I heard these people in the open air; and now, thank God, I am on my way with them to Heaven."

Such a man is not likely to shirk the work, no matter how hard it may be. Amidst the wintry blast and the teeming shower of rain, as well as in the sunshine, feeling how useful and necessary the work is for the thousands who are still just what he used to be, he is likely always to take pleasure in using the means which proved effectual in his own case, and his constant confidence in God's approval of these methods, and of the prospect of their success, will prevent his discouragement amidst the wearying progress of toil which must so often seem to accomplish nothing.

For it is no easy matter to reach the masses with the Gospel, even under the most favourable conditions possible. There must be daily, unwearied, insatiable diligence. There must be constant sacrifice of ease and comfort, and ceaseless exertion of all the powers of mind and body. There must be readiness gladly to endure shame, scoffing, opposition, abuse, and even personal violence at times. In short, the only labourers likely to succeed at all in this desperate undertaking are such as have their hearts wholly set upon its prosecution, and are ready to take any steps whatsoever, or to bear anything whatsoever, that may be necessary.

" But this is making a denomination—a new sect."

Well, and supposing that it is. Is there any harm in doing so ? Is there not a need for just such a " sect " in many a city and town of this kingdom where no such work is being done amongst the masses ? '

But we deny that we are in any proper sense a sect. We refuse to settle down into places of worship such as might be agreeable to our people and their families, but insist upon the open-air stand and the place of amusement where there may be little comfort, but where the most good may be done. We refuse to allow evangelists to stay very long in any one place, lest they or the people should sink into the relationship of pastor and flock, and look to their mutual enjoyment and advantage rather than to the salvation of others. The whole Mission is kept in its course by the direction of one controlling will, and each station is placed under the management of the evangelist stationed there. The evangelists are stationed and removed simply with a view to the general interests of the work. We refuse utterly to allow of any authoritative assembly, committee, church meeting, or any other representative or popular gathering, except purely for the purpose of auditing finance and accepting and confirming and arranging for the execution of the plans which have been tried and proved most calculated to promote the common object. We are not, and will not be made a sect. We are a corps of volunteers for Christ, organized as perfectly as we have been able to accomplish, seeking no church status, avoiding as we would the plague every denominational rut, in order perpetually to reach more and more of those who lie outside every church boundary.

Owing to our adherence to this rigid military system, we are losing almost every year evangelists, as well as people, who, having lost their first love, begin to hanker after the "rights," "privileges," "comforts," "teaching," or "respectability" of the churches. No one remains with us, or is likely to remain, whose sole object in life is not the attainment of the one purpose ever kept before the Mission —the rescue from sin and hell of those who are farthest from God and righteousness. And we only wish to keep such people together. No one can possibly object to the formation of another sect more strongly than we do. Let all who wish to be members of a denomination flee from our borders. We only desire to form and to keep up outside every denominational circle a body as large as we can of free-shooters, for the express purpose of assaulting with spiritual weapons those who, like ourselves, are without the church, but who, unlike us, are still in rebellion against God.

III. The Mission succeeds by teaching converts to be holy.

Not content with merely setting before sinners the way of

salvation from the guilt, power, and punishment of sin, the Mission has constantly pointed out to its converts that full salvation which Jesus has been expressly declared to offer to His people, so that they " being delivered out of the hands of their enemies, might serve Him without fear in holiness and righteousness before Him all the days of their life."

The spiritual children of the Mission have been taught to trace every evil thought and word and deed back to the innate corruption of the heart, and to pray in faith for the instant removal of these inward roots of bitterness, which, springing up, have troubled them. They have been led, thank God, in many instances, " to lay aside," at the feet of Jesus, every weight, and the sin that so easily beset them, and then, leaving all these things behind, to press on to the mark of the prize of their high calling of God in Christ Jesus. Glory be to God, there are many bounding souls amongst us who can sing not merely with reference to the burden of guilt and condemnation, but with regard to every weight that their loving hearts ever felt, whether of evil, of anxiety, or fear, or trouble, or doubt—

> " I left it all with Jesus long ago,
> All my sins I brought Him and my woe ;
> When by faith I saw Him on the tree,
> Heard the still small whisper ' 'Tis for thee,'
> From my heart the burden rolled away.
> > Happy day ! "

With a good and true foundation thus laid, it is easy to love God with all one's heart and soul and mind and strength, and one's neighbour as oneself. " Thy will be done on earth, as it is done in heaven," is a simple matter of fact request which can be as simply realized as " Give us this day our daily bread," once the Holy God has really set up His kingdom in the heart. And this heavenly experience we have very good reason to believe many have not only been taught and led to expect, but have actually attained, in

K

connection with the Mission. Thanks be unto God which giveth us the victory, through our Lord Jesus Christ.

Need we say that the teaching of holiness in the mission has had a very practical direction ? The people have been taught, not so much to seek for rhapsodies of delightful feeling, or sweet, comfortable calm (though these have been preciously enjoyed), as for that perfect love which casteth out fear and fits people for desperate warfare against sin, for that consuming zeal which uses up in the Master's service every faculty and hour. Entire consecration has not been an affair of the drawing-room or the altar of prayer merely. It has been fulfilled upon the high places of the field, where the men of Israel have spent themselves until death has finished their sacrifice of body, soul and spirit to God. We have no patience with that higher life which towers into regions of sublime superiority, leaving God and the world no richer by its attainments. But surely the people of God will not be deluded into forgetting the possibility of the "higher life" of Mount Calvary. In *that* holiness of Jesus, thank God, many of the members of the Mission have lived and died. And their teaching and influence have exercised upon those who have followed the Master at some distance a most blessed and useful effect. To this teaching and experience of holiness is undoubtedly to be ascribed the unquenchable vitality and irrepressible vivacity which have always distinguished some of the oldest stations of the Mission especially.

To teach practical holiness is to teach abstention from drink, and tobacco, and showy dress, and worldly books and amusements.

Nobody can attempt to do good to the working-classes without being met at every turn by the demon drink. The steps of every poor person, from their very childhood, are beset with these gilded traps and nets of hell, and an immense portion of the revenue of this Christian country, and of its churches, flows from the denuded homes of its drunken, blighted, miserable ones whose numbers must daily swell as the youth of both sexes grow up to believe themselves wanting in dignity and position, if they are not the frequent customers of some vendor of the national beverage. We cannot imagine anyone knowing the people, and professing to care about them, while tampering with this most infectious of plagues.

But indeed the Mission, as a rule, has little need to press upon its converts the abandonment of this horrible stuff, for so many of them have smarted from the serpent's bite, and so generally felt is the conviction that going to heaven means leaving off drink, that almost without the mention of any pledge, converts declare their determination to have done with liquor, and the man who breaks his pledge or touches the drink, even if he have nòt been pledged at all, generally concludes at once that it is all over with his religion, and unless picked up at once falls down altogether.

As to tobacco and snuff, the views of many are undoubtedly more cloudy. There is no great harm in it, surely ; but it is so closely linked in the general experience with drink, that it generally has to suffer simultaneous execution for keeping such company. It is waste of money, defilement of breath and person, a feature of likeness to the world, a bad habit bringing up memories of many worse ones, a low practice, beneath the dignity of a man of God, a doubtful thing at best, often causing darkness and doubt in the soul. The Mission has made war upon it, and rescued the most of its people from its enthralling practices and power.

"After I was converted, thinks I to myself one day," said a converted tinker, "I can't find in God's word that Christ nor His Apostles either smoked or snuffed. No more won't I ! So here goes, and I smashed my pipes and put my tobacco a-back o'the fire."

Said another, "I had a controversy for months about my tobacco. I kept asking the Lord to show me His will ; but I knew it all the time, only I felt as if I should like Him to make it the other way. Every time I knelt down to pray this thing would come up, and I could get no rest about it. So at last I said 'I'll have no more of this.' I wrapped up all my pipes in a bit of paper, and put them in my pocket, and walked down to the river. As I walked along I put to my hand and smashed them all in my pocket. That was the sweetest music I ever heard! I asked the Lord to take away the appetite for it, and bless His name I have never felt a desire for a pipe since."

The Mission has taught its converts, women especially, to strip off their ornaments, and dress as becometh women professing godliness.

" As I came out to-night to get myself some things," said a sufficiently well-dressed servant girl the other day, " I found all at once my purse was gone. I have lost five shillings ; but it's all right, I'm sure it will be for the best. Anyway I have got my soul blessed, and that is better than anything I could have got."

The evangelist replied, " Oh ! that a lot of sisters might have their purses stolen when they come out to get things. What a lot of pride and soul-damage would be spared them ! "

The next week she came and said, " I am going home to strip all the feathers and flowers off my bonnet and things, and to make my hat quite plain. I know they will all be on to me about it as soon as ever I begin ; but when they see me stripping off these things and dressing plain, they'll all know my religion is real ! "

No one but those who mix daily with such people can have any idea of the extent to which the dress question enters into their thoughts, and the degree to which the desire for display and admiration menaces the existence of heavenly mindedness. When a young woman has ceased to care whether her things look as fine as Miss Fashion's servants, she has risen above a whirl of ceaseless worry and selfishness, which is most destructive to true peace and rest.

Mission people are generally too eager to get to services to care much for any other employment of their leisure. Each annual holiday is filled up with festivals and special services, which are looked forward to just as the country excursion, or the pantomime, or the bean-feast used once to be. But the Mission has always emphatically taught that separation from the world meant complete estrangement, not only from their unquestionably vicious gatherings and destruction of unquestionably bad publications, but the avoidance of even apparently innocent scenes and literature which might imply evil or worldly associations or communications, which might have about them the appearance of evil, which might lead into temptation, or which might endanger perfect peace with God.

" My people wanted me very badly to go with them to the Crystal Palace to-day, and they couldn't make it out because I wouldn't go with them," said a young convert. " I knew they would be drinking and carrying on, and I wasn't going with them. I said I'd rather stop at home alone all day. They said I would soon go mad with my religion altogether, but I don't care. I'd rather go mad and have Christ than keep my senses and not have Him. So I have had a blessed day, singing and praying all alone."

In short, the Mission has taught its converts that, the Judge being at the door, we ought to pay no regard whatever to the fashion of this world, which passeth away, or to the opinions of dying men and women, but ought to be such manner of persons as in all holy conversation and godliness dare look for, and hasten unto, the coming of the Lord with confidence of not being ashamed before Him at His coming.

IV. The Mission succeeds by teaching its hearers to do their utmost towards meeting the expenses of the work.

The cost of hiring the buildings used, and of maintaining the evangelists and their families in the circumstances they have been accustomed to as working people, has been increasingly contributed to by those who have attended the services, and only supplemented by the liberality of Christian friends throughout the country, who have appreciated the opportunity of helping those who were thus diligent in helping themselves ; so that, during one year, more than £4,000 are received from the poor, as against £3,000 given by the rich. We think it a vastly important test of the value of any work done amongst the poor, to what extent they themselves help to keep it up.

We say to a congregation, "You cannot spend ten minutes in a public-house or music-hall without paying dearly for it, and we are sure, if you like to come here, you will also like to help us to meet the expenses."

We say to a converted man, "Before your conversion, drink and tobacco and sinful pleasure cost you many a bright shilling. Now render unto the Lord some return for all that religion saves you." And to a converted woman, "Now that you don't want artificial flowers, and jewels, and finery with which to adorn yourself, you can afford to help us in the expense incurred in decking our Saviour's crown with stars for ever."

We cannot see how any considerable effort is to be made for the people without large help from themselves ; nor can we see how any large amount of devotion to God can be developed in the hearts of people who are not taught liberally and practically to support His cause.

When a poor woman one evening, after telling how she and her two children had been brought to the very verge of starvation, but had got one day's work and the promise of another the next, and how she could trust God for the future day by day, laid down a penny, probably her very last, to further the cause of God, everyone present felt that her heart was firm, trusting in the Lord ; and, thank God ! we have tangible evidence that the Mission has gathered thousands of such people out of the world for Christ !

CHAPTER XII.

HOW MISSION PEOPLE DIE.

IT has always been accepted as one test, and by no means an insignificant one, of the value of a man's faith that, when the shadows of time are fading from his sight, and the solemn realities of eternity are crowding in, faith shall prove a substance, and shall supply such perfect evidence of things as yet unseen, that the dying man shall see beyond all the gloomy prospects which lie before him and his family and friends, something so glorious as to give light and peace and joy at eventide.

To a poor man or woman, whose earthly prospect has never been very brilliant, whose very bread has been somewhat uncertain from day to day, and whose family have been entirely dependant, humanly speaking, upon the one frame which is now wasting and dissolving, death is especially sad. The bitter question, "What is to become of these little children?" *will* come, and it would be no mean thing if faith, struggling as though itself were dying, could only with a last gasp say, "Thy will be done. I will trust, and not be afraid." Wretched, indeed, for the poor sinner who in such an hour sees even the care for loved ones overshadowed by the awful question, "What is to become of *me?*" And there are many millions of such deaths here in England!

But thanks be unto God, who giveth us the "victory through our Lord Jesus Christ," it has been our privilege to witness and record the deaths of multitudes of poor people whose final moments it has been no ordinary blessing to look upon. Not mere hanging, desperate trust ; not only a quiet peace that death itself could not shake ; but a triumph far surpassing all the triumphs of life—such has been the experience of many a Mission death-bed. Weeping friends, even amidst the sorrow of bereavement, have frequently been compelled to say " it *was* good to be there."

It is no easy matter to represent on paper the joy which words can never express, and scenes so extraordinary, considering especially the circumstances and surroundings of the actors, that any one of them may well linger for ever in the memory as the brightest of a lifetime. We will try, however, to present a few of the most recent, which encourage us still to seek to gather wanderers home to God.

In many cases it is only the close approach of death which induces people to have anything to say to us, and, although we are always unwilling to attach too much importance to such eleventh hour repentances, there are cases in which the genuineness of the work is so satisfactorily demonstrated that we can rejoice without trembling.

Here lies a poor man in a Whitechapel attic upon the floor, with hardly any covering. He scarcely needed to tell his visitor, " Oh, sir, I am dying ! "

" Do you feel Jesus precious ? Has He pardoned your sins?"

" I believe, but—" a dreadful gasp, and then the awful confession that his belief is only of the mental kind that brings no help. He has no conscious connection with the Christ, every word of whose story he fully believes.

But, thank God, before the visitor leaves him, after prayer, and pointing the poor, weary, heavy laden one to the Saviour, he is able to say, "Now, sir, I have no fear of death. May God bless you for coming to see me."

The next morning he passed away, saying, " I am happy. Jesus is precious. I die in peace."

A wretchedly ignorant man, who had spent seventy-one years in heaping up sin of every kind, and who had very often joined in ridiculing the open-air services, sent from his death-bed for some of those whom not long before he used to call "mad fools" to come and pray with him. They were soon there, and had the unspeakable joy, ere long, of seeing their former enemy at peace with God.

Twenty minutes before he died he whispered, " The tide is flowing," no doubt alluding to the *crimson* tide we so often sing about, and soon after, when told the time, he said, " In five minutes I shall be in heaven. I am washed in the Blood."

Sometimes conversion takes place while the sinner is yet to all appearance in health and strength ; but death, coming unexpectedly, prevents our having much evidence of the reality of the change beyond that which comes from dying lips. But some of those cases are far from being the least interesting or satisfactory.

A young man came, by pressing invitation, to a theatre service. The Word took hold of him. Rushing up to the front, he cast himself down before God, pleaded earnestly for mercy, and soon went on his way rejoicing. He ran home, and said—

" Oh, mother, I have got converted to-night, and I am so happy ; but *won't* my mates laugh at me to-morrow ? "

The Lord provided a way of escape from the storm he dreaded. That very night he was seized with an illness, which, in a few days, ended his career.

Another young man—caught and saved from amongst the wild, godless throng of Sabbath-breaking, blaspheming roughs, who frequent the neighbourhood of our Shoreditch Hall, himself as rough as any—was very suddenly called away. He was taken ill on the Tuesday, and died two days later. But he left this blessed testimony with a companion—

" It's all right, mate ; I'm not afraid to die. Jesus is mine."

A poor woman, a cripple, living upon her pittance of 3s. 6d. per week, was led to Christ, and, hobbling about with sticks or crutches, she set to work with all diligence to carry the glad tidings of salvation to others. Four men were known to have been converted as a result of her labours, and how many more she sought to turn from the error of their ways we cannot tell. God knows all about it. But very shortly weakness and sickness increased, and the humble soldier of the Cross passed away, declaring that the blood of Jesus cleansed her from all sin, and urging all around to meet her in Heaven.

A young man who came into one of our halls, one Saturday evening, was smitten with the Spirit's sword, and then made happy in the pardoning love of God. The next week he was laid low with smallpox. But just before they carried him to the hospital, where he died, he said to a friend, " Bless the Lord ! I am glad that ever I saw you. I am glad that I went to the Temperance Hall. I am going to the hospital ; but *it's all right !* "

Gladdening, however, as are these testimonies from persons we know little of here, but with whom we confidently look forward to perfect acquaintance hereafter, we rejoice still more in the glorious termination of lives transformed by the power of the Gospel, and which have, for a long time, cheered and helped us.

A poor man, working in a guano factory, who had wandered far from God, heard a sister and her band preaching Christ in the open air. The Word went to his heart, and after hearing them outside repeatedly, he dared to follow to the Hall, where, a fortnight later, while they pleaded with him to prepare for death, so as to meet his darling children in the skies, he yielded himself again to God, and from that night his happy face was rarely missing from any meeting, outside or in, which he could attend.

He made such progress as to be induced to give an address in the Hall one evening. "Home !" was his subject, and he dwelt almost exclusively on the beautiful heaven he was going to. Little did anyone who listened to the happy man now imagine how soon that home would be his for ever.

One evening, illness seized him at the works, so severely that a mate had to lead him home. To this man he said, "I have received my death-blow."

But, thank God, death was no shock to him. He lay for a few days, looking forward with the greatest joy to the brilliant future, and saying, cheerily—

"Jesus is precious : there's not a cloud." He sent the evangelist a message, one day, that he was

"Sweeping through the gates
To the New Jerusalem
Washed in the blood of the Lamb."

and it was the simple truth.

One of those truly venerable women—one of those working men's wives, who, with the love of God in their hearts, amid poverty and trial of every kind, bring up a large family to honest thrift and toil—has gone up to await the children she has trained so well.

Her eldest son, having found Christ at our services, urged his mother to come. She had learned the truth in childhood's days, but, through many years of sin, trial, and wanderings, had forgotten God.

It was no little thing to ask a woman to come into the little wooden shed, against which stones and bricks were frequently thrown and the services in which were often interrupted by the hooting and shouting of roughs outside. But the power of God was there, and this woman, like many more, felt irresistibly drawn to it. She went, and returned home to know no peace till she found it in the Saviour. By day she saw her sins in all their enormity separating between her and

God. At night she dreamt of union with her little ones who had gone to Heaven, or of everlasting separation from them. At length, however, the dark night of sin ended and the light of heaven shone in her heart.

No sooner had she found salvation, than she boldly took her stand with the persecuted few who were so resolutely preaching the Cross. Everyone who attended that little place was noted and hooted at wherever they went. (This is no uncommon experience with the prominent workers of the Mission.) The leader in the work was, of course, especially blessed with the happiness of those " who endure." Factory girls would tie their shawls together and hold him in the folds of the rope thus made while they spat upon him. But our sister used to watch for him on her doorstep as he passed from his work that she might identify herself continually with the cause he advocated, and might cheer him with a hearty " God bless you !" and a wave of the hand.

In the evening she would get to the open-air service, in spite of a godless husband and a raging mob, and would stand like a soldier amidst the hottest fire.

Such was the state of things that a double ring had often to be formed, sisters within, and brothers, with linked arms, outside, to prevent roughs from breaking up the meeting or seizing the leader, whose life was often threatened. This noble woman generally stood praying with her eyes closed, only opening them to pick out some specially outrageous person as a particular object of prayer.

She told one of the worst of them that if he would not desist and yield his heart to God he would be signally punished. Soon after, the man walked into a lime-kiln in a state of intoxication, and lay down to sleep the sleep of death.

The most violent storm of persecution passed away ; but four weary years of sorrow and patient, persevering prayer passed, before our sister could rejoice in the salvation of her husband, who, soon afterwards, passed away to glory. Other

members of the family and strangers owe their salvation to
the faithful labours and prayers of the godly mother.

The last twelve months of her life were full of bodily
weakness and pain—the last three months passed entirely in
bed. But she passed her time in praising God for all His
goodness and in praying that she might be preserved from
murmuring. Even when unconscious of outward things, she
never seemed to wander from the one line of thought which
absorbed all her faculties.

"Do you know where you are?" asked her eldest son,
as she awoke from one of those seasons of darkness one
day.

" I am on the borders of eternity," she replied, " with my
feet in the river of death. I shall soon be at home over
there."

" Can you leave all your children willingly ? "

" Yes."

" And whose care will you leave us all in ? "

"In the care of Jesus. What better friend could I leave
you with ? "

When Mr. Booth called upon her, two days before her
death, she had been lying for some time unconscious, but his
appearance in the room seemed all at once to arouse her,
and she woke exclaiming, " God bless the Mission."

And how could God bless us more than with such women,
to brave the storm and witness for Jesus, and pass calmly
away at the end to an exceeding great reward ? "

Eighteen hundred and seventy-six witnessed a death scene
which equalled in its glory any that the Mission has yet been
able to record.

A poor old navvy has just been speaking in fervent, simple
words to a few poor people in a little room about the mansions in glory and the preparation necessary to be meet for
one. The exhortation finished, each person present, including the children, is spoken to personally, and then he
sits down. In a few moments he is writhing in the agonies

of death ; but filling each moment of consciousness with glowing words. Looking up to Heaven, he says : " Let me go. I be a child of God, and I be happy ; let me go." He then repeats a favourite verse :

> " How happy the man whose heart is set free,
>   The people that can be joyful in Thee ;
>   Their joy is to walk in the light of His face,
>   And still they are talking of Jesus' grace."

And so was he until, an hour later, he entered into everlasting freedom from poverty and pain and sorrow.

CHAPTER XIII.

THE MISSION HOST IN HEAVEN.

As the usual procession marched into the porch of the Whitechapel Hall, one Sunday evening very early in 1877, an aged woman, who was always to be seen at the Sunday evening service, though unable to attend at any other time, was suddenly seen to reel and clutch at the door. She had been especially anxious to be in time that evening, and friends who caught her falling form heard her last words of faith and prayer as they bore her to the vestry. She had been converted in the early years of the Mission, had met in one Sister Collingridge's class, and had clung to Christ amidst the deepest poverty, in spite of the violent opposition of her friends, some of whom were Roman Catholics.

And now, as the congregation sang, led by some converted policemen, who were there to speak that night,

> " Traveller, yonder narrow portal
> Opens to receive Thy form;
> Yes, but I shall be immortal
> In that land without a storm;
> For I'm going, yes, I'm going
> To that land that knows no storm ! "

the happy spirit of dear old Sister Osborne swept through the pearly gates into the New Jerusalem.

Let us try as suddenly to pass away with her for a season, and allow her to lead us through the golden streets and point out to us some of her natural associates in the land of which the Lord hath said unto us, " I will give it you."

"There is Sister Collingridge, who, from being a weak, timid creature, unable to pray in public, became a fearless open-air speaker, a soul-saving preacher in-doors, and an indefatigable visitor amongst the vilest neighbourhoods she could discover. She might well sing, just before she came here—

> ' Oh, I am going to wear that crown,
> To wear that starry crown ; ' "

for she sent a lot in before her—amongst them the poor woman who died singing, ' I love Jesus ! hallelujah ! ' and whose infidel husband was converted, soon after her death, by means of a word or two Mrs. C. had let drop ; and the old Crimean soldier who used to oppose the open-air meetings so, but who, as a result of her visits, died singing—

> ' I on the brink of ruin fell;
> Glory to God, I 'm out of hell ! ' "

"There's Mary Dobson, who came up from the garret where she lived fifteen years with her four children and her husband, who worked there as well. Though she only received the light, and sought the Lord on her bed of death, she got the old navvy downstairs converted before she came away, and made the rough men about sing her hymns of glory as she left them behind. She died a true mission woman, and is one still, I assure you."

"There's Thomas Musgrove, who used to be so fond of theatres, and got converted in one, only three months before he died, and whose dying request to his mother was, ' Dry up your tears, and meet me in heaven ! ' "

"And there's Susan Sadler, who was caught at an open-air service which the police broke up. She got up from her sick bed to go to the open-air meetings as long as she could, and

when she had no more strength left, came away, singing,
'I am ready!—all is well!'"

"Sarah Ann Burrows has fulfilled her dying song—

> ' There's not a cloud that doth arise
> To hide my Saviour from my eyes;
> I soon shall mount the upper skies.
> All, all is well!'

She was caught in the open air, too, sought mercy in a
theatre, and found it in a temperance-hall."

"There's Thomas Hayward, that once was a drunkard,
and only got converted, along with his wife and sister,
five weeks before he had to come off here. It was what you
folks call Good Friday—certainly, a Good Friday to him,
when he came up, saying, 'Praise the Lord!' And, praise
the Lord, we have got his sister-in-law, too, who passed
through years of bodily pain with such joy, and said, 'I am
so happy!' at the end of it all, raising her dying hand in
triumph. The angels have often had to rejoice over sinners
that his wife has broken down with telling about him in the
open air, and hope she will send on many more."

"Mary Brown came from Bethnal Green, too. She was
only brought back from her back-sliding three months before
the end of her life down there. She was able to get to the
hall only a few days before her death, and tell them she was
sure of coming here."

"That young girl of eighteen, who was converted only
eighteen hours before her death, came from Bethnal Green
about the same time."

"Thomas S. Mitchell, who was such a friend of the poor,
but used to doubt so about being saved till he fell in with
your folks, is now quite sure he is safe. It was beautiful—
was it not, to be at work on Tuesday, consulting about work
on Wednesday evening, and safe here on Friday night?"

"And Mrs. M., who lived in such darkness and suffered so
terribly, right up to the last day, with a cancer; but trusted

L

in the Lord, and was delivered from all her fears. Her face 'was lightened,' too was it not, even before she came to shine here for ever ? "

" There's Sister Francis, one of your first converts at that Limehouse Penny Gaff, who got her three children converted, trusted in God when her husband was out of work and they were all likely to starve, and got starved away to us, saying, ' I shall soon prove what that rest is.' She *has* proved what it really is, I can tell you."

" And little Georgie Jenner, who only lived eight years below, and said, when his little feet were in the river, ' Mother, I'm dying ; but I've given my heart to Jesus, and I'm going to heaven ! Will you give your heart to Jesus, mother, and then you will meet me there ? ' "

" Fanny Prong, who used to be so happy, and used to hurry to the meetings late, after her long day's work. Her last song below was—

> ' We'll stand the storm, it won't be long ;
> We'll anchor by and by.'

Her storm only lasted eighteen years, and here she is, safe enough and merry enough for ever now. She anchored about the same time as that poor Whitechapel woman, who had been a backslider for forty years, and sent for your folks from her dying bed. She said she would sing ' unto Him that loved us, and washed us from our own sins in His own blood ;' and you should hear her sing it."

" ' Blessed Jesus, I come to Thee,' Sister Livermore said, as she rose from that bed of agony and want, where you people found her in despair, and sung and prayed her into faith and life. She threw her earthly life away by wickedly departing from the God of her youth ; but still she is here."

" There is that sister from Stoke Newington, whose infidel husband said she should not attend your meetings ; but she was converted there, and she would go, until from her bed of smallpox she rose up here waving her poor hands, and shouting victory through the blood of the Lamb."

"Just about the same time, another smallpox patient from Whitechapel came shouting along. She was one of the first fruits from your great hall, though she heard Mr. Booth in the theatre first. She used to be dreadfully poor when she was with you. But that is all over."

"Another Whitechapel woman, Sister B., who said 'not to-night' when she heard the Gospel, and went to her death-bed without God as the result, was just saved by the visits of your folks at the last. 'O ! Lamb of God, I come,' she said, and came."

"And there's that brother from Stoke Newington, who was converted the first time he came to the hall, and died saying to his wife, 'My dear, meet me in heaven. Give my love to all the dear mission friends, and tell them I am going to be with Jesus.'"

"There's the Tottenham policeman that *would* go back and be saved after the morning service the first time he heard your people, and who, after witnessing for Jesus for sixteen days, broke a blood vessel and joined us."

"There's Sister W., of Globe Road, who was restored from backsliding after hearing a sister preach there, and whose husband was restored as he knelt by her bedside. In another twelve days she came up from the Smallpox Hospital, singing."

"There's Sister L., of Poplar, who was converted after hearing your people in the Oriental Theatre. They said she was mad when she was seeking mercy, and madder still afterwards ; but she kept on speaking for God, and winning souls. They said she was 'unconscious' when she came here, but her last words, 'Blessed Jesus, I believe I shall meet Thee there,' after she had sung, 'Yes, we shall gather at the river,' have proved sober and sensible enough."

"There's Brother B., of Stratford, who lost religion for a godless young woman, and found it again at your hall. He did all the preaching he could, and with all his might, too, till the smallpox landed him here."

"And there's that William Rose! What a profligate wretch he was when he came to the free breakfast, and had all his sins set before him! And what a dreadful time of it he had with the butchers! But, instead of fearing their insults, he preached to them, and led one that had been drinking, thieving, and fighting the night before to Jesus. How he did work for God everywhere, until the machine wheel caught him and flung him up to us, happy!"

"There's Brother Chaffer, of Stoke Newington, who went out to help you as long as he could while dying of consumption, and then, after passing months of weariness, and weakness and pain, in the sweetness and joy of Divine love, slipped away, saying 'I'm going, I'm going. Fetch Jesus. Bless his name!'"

"Brother Dipleck, of Hastings, too, amidst his acutest sufferings, said 'Don't grieve for me. I am going to be with Jesus. Praise His name! Just one five minutes in heaven will make up for all this pain. I shall soon be home.' And so he was!"

"There is Sister Rainsby, of Poplar, the poor dock labourer's wife, who kept house gladly after her conversion on ten and sixpence a week, and said 'I am now better off than my Saviour was on earth, for I have bread, and sometimes he had none.' When dying, blinded by smallpox and weakened by privation, she said 'Though it is dark without, it is light within. Jesus is lighting up the valley. His presence more than repays me for the pangs I feel. Oh, the gates are now opened for my entrance. The angels are waiting. Oh, John! don't you see Jesus? Oh, all is well! I am now going to a world of eternal joy. I am exchanging sorrow and suffering for a crown of eternal life.' And then she did it."

"And there's Sister Smith, the gipsy's wife, who used to bring her little children out with her rather than miss attending an open-air service. When illness suddenly came on she naturally remarked, ' I am very happy. Jesus is very precious. If I die, I feel I shall go to heaven.' She got away so quickly that nobody knew just when she did come. But here she is, sure enough."

" There is Sister H., of Croydon, who endured so much pain so happily, and when dying said, ' What should I do without my hope ? I am in the river Jordan, but I can't sink. Jesus has got me ! It's *real!* It's *real* ! It's all right ! It's all right ! I shall soon be in heaven.' "

" And Sister Shackle, of Canning Town, who when her husband was seized with small pox, while she lay helpless on her bed of languishing, said ' The Lord doth all things well'; and, when she took the malady and lay racked with all sorts of pain, said, ' This is nothing compared with what Jesus suffered for me '; and, when she could not speak out, whispered, ' I bless God for this affliction ! I cannot praise him enough ! Jesus does so wonderfully sustain my soul '. And when dying said, ' I am safe. I shall soon be home. All is well.' "

" There is Sister Probey, of Millwall, who was so fond of the means of grace while she could get out, and testified for Jesus so clearly while she could, that her smiling face as she passed away, too weak to speak, was quite enough to assure everybody that she was coming straight here."

" And that poor woman who was led to Christ while dying of cancer at Poplar, and who said, while her life was being gnawed away. ' I shall soon be where sorrow and suffering are no more. I am happy in Jesus. I have no fear of death.' Just before she started she pointed upwards, unable to tell them where she was going, and then the angels caught her up."

" The Stoke Newington sweep, William King, too, what a drunkard he was when he lay three days on the tap-room floor ! But they caught him in the open air, and when he was converted he gave up drink, tobacco, and all, and went in for God and souls with all his might. No wonder that when somebody asked him on his last day, ' Are you afraid to die ? ' He replied, 'No, bless God, I am going home—heaven's my home.' "

" We have a sister Collins who was brought back to God at Whitechapel, and clung to Him in spite of the persecutions of a drunken, godless husband. She rejoiced amidst long and severe bodily affliction, and insisted upon sending two shillings of the little she had to help the cause of God a few days before her death, saying, ' Oh, it is such an *honour* to give to Jesus.' The words, ' Precious Jesus,' were on her lips when they raised her up and carried her here."

" Bro. Hipple, too, whose preaching was blessed to so many, was commending his soul to Christ when they took him up."

" Brother Manning, who had lived fifty-three years in sin, when he was brought to God in that hall near Mile End Gate, that used to be a public-house, lifted up his hands and said, ' Come, Lord Jesus ! Come, my precious Jesus ! All is well. I shall soon be home. No suffering there. We shall meet there. Farewell ! ' and followed sister Collins, his old class-mate, who was only a few days before him, to fellowship up here for ever."

" Sister Clarke, the first-fruits of Tunbridge Wells, was poor enough in the lower world. The parish buried her body. But she was converted in that wooden shed, and could truly say when asked how she was on her dying bed, in that wretched little place, ' Oh, all right—only my head is bad. But it is all for the best. The Lord does all things well,'—and did well to add, when her mother said :

" ' Oh, but she looks very sadly,' "

" ' I shan't be sadly long, mother. I shall soon be better off.' So she is, and no mistake."

" Sister Beal, the first-fruits of Wellingbro', followed her closely. She had a dreadful fortnight of conviction before she found peace ; but she testified publicly for Jesus the evening after, and five weeks later was with us here."

" Brother Barber, of Shoreditch, with whom they had to
go from the City of London Theatre to the Mission Hall at
half-past ten one Sunday evening because he was in such an
agony of conviction, and would not go home without Christ.
He fought hard for his new Master ever after till sudden
illness laid him low. His dying testimony was as glorious
as his life :

" 'It's a reality. I see the angels and hear the heavenly
music. Jesus is precious. It's better on before ! Lord
Jesus come quickly ! I've had a battle ; but have gained
the victory ! Oh, death, where is thy sting ? I shall soon
sit down at the marriage feast. Glory to God ! I see a
light ! Lord Jesus, receive my soul !' "

" I wonder if his sister and all present are taking the advice
he gave when she said, ' I shall soon follow you. ' "

" ' Don't be in a hurry. Work for the Master.' "

" Brother Garnish, of Whitechapel, too, big rough navvy as
he was, was caught in a Theatre and converted in the hall,
along with his wife. He made his godless fellow-workmen see
and acknowledge that he was a new man in Christ Jesus,
and died saying, ' I know that my Redeemer liveth. The
precious blood ! ' "

" Brother Stevens, of Bethnal Green, was convinced of sin
by the singing of a missioning band while he sat at his fireside
one Sunday evening, and dared not sleep without Christ,
because the words of a sister, ' You may be dead, damned,
and in hell before morning,' would not leave his mind till he
got up and in his bedroom found salvation. He was called
away suddenly ; but could sing, ' If ever I loved thee, my
Jesus, 'tis now,' upon his dying bed, and he can sing it
better still up here."

" We have got some charming little children from the
Mission too. Those two Limbachs, for instance. Emma,
who died after three and-a-half years on the earth, singing,
' Safe in the arms of Jesus,' and Fred, ten years old, who
used to distribute tracts, ' For the Lord,' who died a few

days after his sister, shouting, 'Glory! I am going home! Wait a minute, Emma, I'm coming!'"

"There's Billy Ferris, of Limehouse, who used to be such a drunken, fighting fellow, until he got saved. He worked for God as only a navvy could, afterwards, and yet was not satisfied, for he said to one of his mates, 'I mean to try to be more like Jesus than ever,' only an hour before the tub of ballast fell upon him, and sent him flying up here."

"There's Mother Fowler, of Whitechapel, who was a drunkard when she heard Mr. Booth preach on the Mile End Waste. Who ever missed the poor old woman from a service afterwards? They scarcely ever brought anybody from a poorer home; but here she is."

"There's Sister Willis, the first-fruits of the Hastings Mother's Meeting, who used to scoff so when she first heard the Gospel (and no wonder, considering the dreadful life she had led); but who said, when they asked if she would trust Jesus in the valley of death, 'Yes; for He'll be with me.' He brought her safe through."

"There's Arthur Bridges, the first-fruits of Chatham, who sang so loudly on his death-bed when he got his sister to Jesus, that they heard him in the next street. He was a missioner, and no mistake, and came away singing, 'One by one they're passing over;' and shouting, 'I have the victory! Glory, hallelujah!'"

"He was soon followed by dear old Father Barber, of Stratford, who was such a drunken, immoral wreck when he stepped into that little place near the Canal Bridge to hear a woman preach. How he stuck to it ever after, and how he loved and cared for everybody there while his wife and family abused him so for going! No wonder he was so happy upon his bed of pain. 'All light—light, joy, peace!' in spite of the people about him, so full of glory he 'must burst with its weight.' He has larger capacity now."

"There is Brother Richardson, of Southsea, who used to spend his Sundays in amusement till he heard Mrs. Booth in the Portland Hall, and writhed under conviction, so that two men had to hold him up. He did what he could for God ever after, till sudden sickness swept him away, and then died singing—

> ' The precious blood of Jesus, it washes white as snow ;
> Lord, I believe it, for Thou hast washed me.
> Shout, shout the victory ! I'm on my journey home.'

He waved his hands to the tune, and, when he could sing no more, whispered, ' All is well ! all is well !' and was here."

"Brother Young, of Whitechapel, is another of Mrs. Booth's children, who at the last sang, ' There'll be no more sorrow there !' and said, ' I am going home.' "

"Brother Mills, of Portsmouth, who preached so boldly at the street corners in all weathers, and warned his dockyard mates so faithfully as long as he could, came away crying, ' Salvation's free ! Oh, the blood of Jesus cleanseth me !' "

"His brother Ings, of Buckland, came off so suddenly and quietly that he had not time to say a word ; but he had fully proved that his conversion was real before he was laid up."

"Brother Abercrombie, of Whitechapel, was a holy man, and when he cried out, ' Come again, Jesus ! Oh, come again, blessed Jesus !' Jesus went and brought him home."

"His Sister Lemas told them with a smile, when they asked if she was afraid to die, ' No ; I am going to Jesus.' Just like a woman, to save Him the trouble of coming for her ! "

"Brother Spain, of the Royal Marines, who was converted along with his wife at the Chatham Lecture Hall, and sanctified too, and who led so many of his comrades to Christ, said like a soldier, when he heard the hospital people say, ' Spain is dying,' ' Yes, but I'm not afraid.' He had no need to be *then*, though, as he used to say, if he had died in Ashantee, he would have gone to hell."

"There's Brother Bollard, of Kettering, who tried to sing, 'With steady pace the pilgrim moves towards the blissful shore,' at the last, and when he found he could not sing, he smiled and said, ' 'Tis better on before.' He *can* sing now."

"There's Sister Hazel, of Soho, who wandered from her God until your visitors found her dying, and led her back to Him, so that she could say, 'I see the way now. I see Jesus ;' and could sing—

> 'Sweeping through the gates to the new Jerusalem,
> Washed in the blood of the Lamb.'"

"There's Brother Parkes, of Hastings. He got turned out of one home after another for having meetings and getting people converted, till God found him a permanent mansion. He might well say at the end, 'Won't it be nice to get home ?' But his life and sufferings were 'nice' to him, too ; for he said when his wife read, 'Thy will be done,' 'Oh, that is nice ! I feel I am folded up in His arms, doing His will on earth. Praise the Lord ! I only want to do His will !'"

" But Sister Russell, of Hastings, got here five days before him. She was saved as she sat on her seat in the Market Hall, but went to the penitent form afterwards just to please God ; and, after four years of faithfulness and suffering, could say, 'I am all right. Whether I live or die, I am the Lord's. I feel I am in the valley of the shadow of death now ; but Christ is precious to me.'"

"Sister Jackson, of Croydon, suffered long and severely, too ; but she was a soldier-witness even in her bed-room to the last. 'Yes ; but you know the blood of Jesus Christ cleanseth from *all* sin,' she said to somebody who didn't believe it, and, stepping across the room to get her Bible to prove this, she fell in a fit, and was taken up and brought home here."

" Brother Moody, of Southsea, was sadly reckless and careless till he went out of curiosity to hear a woman preach

Then he became careless of himself in serving the Lord, and had a right to say at the end of it, ' The gates of the city will be open, and I shall go through shouting, Victory ! ' "

" Brother Davis, of Poplar, said to his wife, as on their usual Sunday morning's walk they passed the Hall, ' How they *do* sing ! Let 's go inside.' It was well they did ; for they both got converted ; and, after living for God and pleading in tears ' like a brother ' with his mates to seek the Lord, he asked almost at the last minute if there were any sinners in his room to preach to. ' If so, God sent His only-begotten Son into the world to die for them. He died for me. I am all right.' When they asked if he could see Jesus, he answered, ' Yes ; He is going through the streets of Jerusalem with His banner, Victory, Victory ! and, after praying as long as his breath would last, finished up and came away with an 'Amen.' "

" Sister Ward, of Croydon, after five years service could say as she lay ' unconscious,' and unable to recognize any earthly friend, when asked if she knew the Lord Jesus, pointing with her hand, ' He is there, looking at me all the while,' and recovered sufficiently to sing

> ' Joyful, joyful will the meeting be
> When from sin our hearts are pure and free,
> And we shall gather, Saviour, with Thee
> In our eternal home,'

just before she came to it."

" There is a Sister Winner, the first fruits of Middlesbro', the pleasure seeker who heard the truth in the theatre with her husband, and after enjoying the true pleasure with him for three months, fell asleep saying, ' I am dying but washed in the blood.' ' I'm going to heaven.' ' You will meet me there.' ' Live nearer to God.' "

" There's Brother Pounds, of Poplar, who could not sing much, happy as he was while he lived, but sang when dying so wonderfully, that his neighbours came to see what it meant."

"There is Sister Robertson, of Whitechapel, who died saying, 'Talk of the gates ajar, why I can see them wide open —wide open—open for me. I see the King. He is beautiful! He is lovely! Oh they were to give me a linsey dress—but what a poor one to the one I will get. I will be clothed in whiteness—beautiful dress.'"

"And there's Bob Clark, of Poplar, who used to be as rough a navvy as ever drank or fought, till he got converted, and made his mates say, 'If there is such a thing as religion, Bob Clark's got it.' What a man he was to preach in the open-air, to be sure, in his working clothes, alone or anyhow! His wife was a terrible trouble to him till he got her brought back to God, just before they both died. They both lay in their little cottage unable to help one another, and she came up three weeks before him, saying, 'Oh they're singing so beautiful. They're singing, "My rest is in heaven; my rest is not here." Bless God I can sing it too. I'm going, good-bye, God bless you all.'"

"Bob said, though left unable to wait on himself, with three motherless children, 'Though He slay me, yet will I trust in Him.'"

"When his little daughter told him he was dying, he said, 'No, my dear, this can't be dying that people so much dread.' Five minutes before the end, however, he added, 'I *am* now. Good-bye! God bless you!'"

"Henry White, the first man fully employed in the work who came here, was a blessed saint. He worked in the Victoria Docks, and warned his mates faithfully, and rejoiced in poverty and hardships. When he had that fall down the ship's hold and broke his ribs, and they asked him how he felt, he said, 'Oh praise the Lord if its sudden death, it's sudden glory.' What a lot of people he led to Christ and set to work on that Canning Town Bridge open-air stand! How he used to pray! The Sunday before he died, he said, 'Tell them on the bridge I am going to heaven, but I haven't gone in silver slippers. I have come through floods of trial, but the Lord has brought me through.' And the next Saturday he was brought through, waving his hands in triumph."

" Brother Valentine, of Barking, to which place brother White pioneered the Mission way, was a wretched, broken-hearted backslider when he was saved in that little Bethel up the stairs. Two months later, after witnessing for Jesus outside and in, at work and at home, he came up crying, 'I am going to heaven, shouting victory through the blood of the Lamb, trampling the enemy under my feet.' "

" We have Brother Cooper, the converted infidel, of White-chapel, who was so happy to proclaim Jesus outside and in, after he was caught in the East London Theatre while trying to criticise the preacher. When unable any longer to testify in public himself, he sent from his bed of death the message, 'Tell them I know the blood of Christ cleanseth from all sin. Tell them it can, and it does, there's no supposing or perhapsing about it. *I know, I know.'* "

" And there's Mother Gwennell, of Stratford, that endured such dreadful convictions night and day for weeks, till she came, and was enabled to shout, 'I am saved.' What courage she got to come to the open-air and in-door services, amidst the raging mobs that used to hoot and pelt everybody! She persevered to the end, and then sent word to the hall, 'Tell them I'm almost home.' It is not *almost* now."

"And Sister Goodhew, of Barking, that came up from such poverty, saying that her hope was ' built on nothing less than Jesus' blood and righteousness.' "

" Sister Hague, of Middlesbro', had very nearly perished after having found salvation in the Theatre, and wandered again from God; but she returned to Him again on her death bed, and could say, 'I am very happy, and know I shall soon be in heaven,' a little before she got here."

" There's Brother Walker, of Limehouse, that used to clap his hands and laugh for joy amongst his godless mates, while he said, ' The blood of Jesus cleanses me from all sin *now*—not yesterday or some other time since, but *now*.' When the falling spar hurried him off here, he could well say, ' I'm not afraid to die. All is well.' "

" And praying John Smith. What a blessed happy old saint he was, when he took off his coat to preach on Battle Green, and jumped, and laughed, and clapped his hands everywhere about Jesus ! No wonder he should come away all at once, saying, ' I be a child of God, and I be happy. I do love God. Let me go, Bless ye. I be happy.' "

" Fred Goddard, of Limehouse, that used to be such a wild young man till he was caught in that old hall, was not long behind him. He spoke out for God while he could, and while the smallpox was hurrying him off here, laughed and said, ' Happy ! Yes, I should think I am. Why I'm going to heaven, of course I am.' "

" Then came Brother Cobet, the Mission gentleman, who toiled about when scarcely fit to be up at all, spending all his leisure moments in collecting and similar work, for the Croydon station. He was allowed to conclude all his business arrangements in the orderly way he liked, before he came away crying, ' It's all praise now. It's all praise now.' "

" Sister Lainson, of Portsmouth is here too, who was saved in that great music hall where so many have been ruined, and in the blindness of her last hours was asked, ' Is Jesus precious now ? ' ' Oh, *so* precious—precious. It is all light—glorious—light. Heaven is opened,' she replied, and just before her body fell back dead, sang, ' Hallelujah, Hallelujah, Praise ye the Lord.' "

" And poor Elizabeth Booth, the servant-girl, who, as she lay dying of smallpox, beat time to the songs of Zion with her poor leprous hands, and praised God as well as her swollen lips and tongue would allow, is safe here too."

" Sister Young, of Rye, who ran out to help the first Mission man she ever saw in the street, and spoke the moment she was asked, caught a cold in the open air, which has landed her here after only twenty-eight years down below. Earthly people call that very sad, do they not ? "

" There is Sister Eden, of Wellingbro', who just came to the place and got saved a week before the fever which sent her here took hold of her. Her last words, ' I shall soon be at rest on Jesu's breast,' are gloriously realized now, are they not ? "

" There is Brother Crowhurst, of Whitechapel, whom everybody loved so. Before he was converted, he used to be so fond of theatres and music-halls, that he could scarcely ever spend an evening at home ; but afterwards he became so fond of the work of God, that he not only spent Sundays and week evenings at it, but often eat his dinner as he ran along the streets, in order to spend a little time at noon-day services. No wonder he could happily say ' It is all right' when smallpox suddenly transferred him to us."

" Sister Dolly, of Croydon, who was so happy while she lay in the infirmary wracked with pain, followed her husband here just about the same time."

" It was at Croydon that Sister Anderson, the first of your evangelists who joined us here, spent the last of her strength for Christ. What a trouble it was to her to speak at first ! But, oh, how earnestly she lived and spoke for Jesus towards the end ! A lonely, despised female preacher. Just look where they have put her now ! "

" The smallpox cut off young Jones, of Hackney, from life with you very early. But perhaps his parting words, ' Never mind what men say—never mind what shopmates say—oh, this is beautiful—this is glorious ! ' may be blessed to thousands yet."

" And, oh, was it not glorious when Sister Atkins, of Whitechapel, after serving God and labouring for souls amidst so much poverty and sickness for so many years, came away, saying, 'Jesus is precious!'"

"Her Sister Sherwood, of Whitechapel, came here quite suddenly. It was well that she had her lamp trimmed and ready at a moment's call."

"And Brother Wheatley, of Whitechapel, had not much longer warning. But a man who could say when they thought him only half conscious and asked if he knew Jesus, 'I should think *I do* know in whom I believe,' was not to be caught unawares. Here he is."

"Brother Wells, of Whitechapel, was not sick long either. He rushed up, shouting, 'Glory, glory, glory!' Oh, bless you, no! Nobody objects to that kind of thing here."

"There is Sister Tremlett, of Leeds, who used to be so fond of pointing seeking souls to Jesus, both at Middlesbro' and Leeds, and who could say when dying, 'This is not a dark valley, but it's all light. It's rising higher and higher.'"

"No wonder that Sister Hunt, of North Ormesby, after her long illness, said, when they told her she would soon come here, 'I don't mind if it's to-morrow.' She had got the sort of religion that makes people certain where they are going, and she was quite right when she told her nurse angels were waiting to carry her home. 'There they are, all dressed in white,' she said. 'Good-bye.' And here she is."

"Squire Woodhead, the little Bradford lad, sung and prayed like a proper Mission chap as long as he had breath to do it, and now just look at him!"

"His classmate, William Crabtree, was after him quick. He led his wife to Jesus before he left her to struggle alone. 'Oh, won't it be grand when we all get there!' he said. And so it will."

"There is Brother Bellinger, of Whitechapel, that used to open his shop on Sundays till he began to attend the dear old Hall. He died in a state of unconsciousness, but he

had previously assured his wife that his sins were all
forgiven, and that he was coming straight off here."

" And there is Thomas Dilks, the happy carman, who used
regularly to spend his Sunday mornings in fighting before
he learnt to fight for Jesus. 'Yes; let's dash into it!'
he said, the last time he was asked to help at an open-air
service. And it was not long before he came dashing in
here at a speed they don't let you drive at in London."

" Little did your Whitechapel folks think when Bro.
Thomas, their evangelist, struggled out, looking so ill that
stormy wet evening, to the funeral service of Bro. Dilks,
and dared to announce himself to preach the funeral sermon
of Bro. Bellinger the next Sunday, that he would so soon
come away here himself. But he raised up a lot of recruits
to follow in the front rank, before the heart disease hurried
him off so suddenly that Tuesday evening. No man ever
had a happier time amongst you, but that is nothing to the
blessed eternity we have got here together."

" But there, bless you, there's lot's more ; you won't
know the names nor the faces of one in a hundred, if I
were to show you them. Good-bye. Go and send us some
more. No end of people come through your services that
you know nothing about. We shall be glad to see you
again some day."

Reader, you mean with us to join this company by and
by. But, oh ! remember that the associates of time will be
the associates of eternity. Do not hope to mingle with the
happy throng around the throne if you run with the
multitude to do evil below. You may never be able to see
or to help us here below (though we do not hesitate to say
you ought to help us if you can). But you can meet us at
the Saviour's feet. You can get your sins washed away in
the all-cleansing fountain. You can help to publish His
salvation to your dying fellow-men. You can cheer and
aid your fellow-travellers to the new Jerusalem. And then
we shall meet to render to Him by whom all the good that

M

is done in the earth is done, everlasting thanks, and glory, and honour. Shall we not?

OUR MARSEILLAISE.

YE sons of God, awake to glory,
  A host of foes before you lies;
The saints renowned in sacred story,
  Behold them seize the glittering prize!
Shall frowns of earth or hell's loud thunder
  Afflict your bosom with dismay,
  Or chase you from the narrow way?
While angels gaze with joy and wonder.

    To arms, to arms, ye brave;
    See, see the standard wave.
    March on, march on, the trumpet sounds,
      To victory or death.

The treacherous world stands yonder smiling,
  And points to wealth, delight, and fame;
More venomed than the serpent coiling,
  She leads to anguish, want, and pain.
Fly her embrace, disdain her fury;
  What though her legions she engage?
  From all the follies of her rage
The shield of faith can well secure ye.

March on, nor fear death's sable waters—
  The foe stands silent as a stone,
While Jesus' ransomed sons and daughters
  Go through to claim the promised throne.
White robes and crowns of highest glory,
  Victorious palms and endless songs,
  Victorious palms and endless songs,
And God's bright presence is before ye.

CHAPTER XIV.

OUR FUTURE, D.V.

THE Mission will always remain under the direction and control of an earthly Commander-in-Chief, called the General Superintendent. Local committees are very useful for the examination of financial affairs, for the making of special arrangements, or the accomplishment of special undertakings at exceptional times; but the superiority of a personal directorate over a divided management has come to be all but universally recognized.

From the mightiest Governments on earth to the smallest business concerns of the village, it has, therefore, come to be a rule, with but few exceptions, that a single will must reign, and one individual bear the great burden of responsibility, if anything worth while is to be accomplished; and to say, "There is no man at the wheel!" is to pronounce the most complete and the most damaging condemnation of any organisation.

By this means, above all, can our members be preserved from the tendency to sectarianism, and kept continually moving on for the fulfilment of the great evangelistic purpose for which alone the Mission exists. The supremacy of one who is pledged to an invariable and unalterable programme is a guarantee for the perpetual prosecution at every station of the same system, which has proved so blessedly successful hitherto.

The Mission will continue to be an organization of the poor, because "not many mighty, not many noble, are called" to such glory and virtue as its labours demand. Its services will always repel people of "taste," while they continue to be so strongly flavoured with the power of the Holy Ghost, and the simple, straightforward truth of God, deeply rooted in willing hearts, and bursting forth in irrepressible exuberance, under the directest rays of the Sun of Righteousness.

Its fearless, daring movements to overthrow sin, in spite of any quantity and variety of opposition, will constantly be condemned by "men of judgment"—that is to say, by men who desire to hold the balance evenly between the opinions of the world and the convictions of the heart, instead of saying, in the mighty words our own God himself has given us, "Let God be true and every man a liar!" Its heavenly testimony to the possibility of perfect purity of heart and life will always insure for it the bitterest opposition of hell.

But God will always find it friends amongst those who have the power to add to its slender financial resources, and who, even if not agreeing with every little detail of its characteristics, will love it and be thankful to help it, for its work's sake. Not that it will ever, in all probability, cease to endure financial embarrassment. The offerings, of its own people, always a proper and satisfactory test of the amount of good they have received from its ministrations, will continue steadily to increase ; but these, supplemented by the generous liberality of some, and the grudging leavings of others, will always be inadequate to meet the demands which its large-hearted and self-sacrificing policy will entail.

Its General Superintendent and others, burning with love to souls, and longing to spend all their hours in purely spiritual work, will continue to be sometimes tied down night and day, to the service of tables, for which, depend upon it, there will be a reckoning with somebody by-and-bye.

But never mind ! The Christian Mission will still go on singing as joyously on earth as in heaven with regard to all its trials and difficulties,

> " When my weakness leaneth on His might,
> All seems light."

Yes, the Christian Mission will fight and win for ever and ever, in spite of earth and hell, doggedly maintaining the struggle against iniquity in some of its most awful strong-holds, rushing forth from time to time into new neigh-bourhoods with the standard of the Cross, and as daringly abandoning in case of need positions found to demand an unfair amount of strength in proportion to the results achieved. We should not like to make any sort of estimate of the proportions it will have assumed, even in another ten years, and if asked to give our reasons for this confidence of hope we would simply say, "The Lord our God will fight for us."

But have we not reason for confidence, looking even at the human elements of success which we possess ?

We have got together hundreds of men and women who are eager to do their very uttermost for God and souls. Of course, a certain period of religious experience is necessary ere these people, generally speaking utterly ignorant of the very theory of salvation before their conversion, are able to take any very large share in the work of leading and teach-ing others. But very many are now beginning to give evi-dence that they possess every needful qualification for the very foremost places in our ranks. We have already no less than thirty-one persons labouring as evangelists in the Mission whom the work itself has produced—most of them having been converted in the Mission, and all having been called from secular employment and trained to evangelistic labour in its midst. Besides these, we have the names of no less than sixty-six others who have been thus raised up by the Mission, and wholly employed in connection with various denominations and missions, as preachers, evangelists, missionaries, bible women, colporteurs, and the like. Others again, who have been connected with the Mission until compelled from some cause to move away to a distance from any of its stations write us from time to time to tell how God is using them in the army, the navy, and in every part of the world, to win souls and glorify God.

And then there are all the Mission children, who are being brought up to regard the saving of souls as the great object of life. Look, for example, at the family of the General Superintendent. How prominently and successfully Mr. Bramwell and Miss Booth are engaged in the work we have shown in these pages. Three other members of the family have already taken part in services, and all the four sons and five daughters look forward to spending their life in the work.

In many a mission family the same grand career is ever kept before boys and girls alike, as the highest summit of earthly greatness to be longed and prayed and sought after. The generals of the future are being reared in the homes of the rank-and-file of to-day.

Now, see what any one of such people can be used to do.

We have again and again sent a man, who could not parse a sentence to save his life, into a large town, where he did not know a single person. He has hired a theatre or music hall, with nobody on the spot to promise a penny towards the rent. He has taken his stand in the open air, and on the stage, and trusting simply in the power of the Holy Ghost to speak the grand old gospel of Christ through his lips, has gathered congregations, led hundreds of sinners to Jesus, and left behind him at the year's end a thoroughly organized and drilled mission, supported very largely by the people of the town. This can be done wherever there is a great working class population and suitable buildings available ; for it must be borne in mind that men of this stamp are not trammelled by any of the difficulties which beset an ordinary preacher. If the people will not in the first instance go to a building, he goes out to them. If when they do come, they are so rough and untrained as to have no idea of the decorum of an ordinary religious service, it does not in the least affect his confidence or enthusiasm, except to increase it, and he goes at them with just such language, arguments, illustrations, and anecdotes as they can understand and appreciate. He has no reputation to sustain, no salary to care about. True he takes an offering towards the expenses, but he is saved from undue anxiety on this score by the assurance that the General Superintendent will see him safely through all the financial obligations necessary to his undertaking. This, of course, is a tower of strength to a man, and not only in the way of finance, but as regards the general direction of his work, he feels that he is sent to carry out a certain programme, and that in any difficulty or emergency that may arise, he can fall back for counsel, sympathy, and support on those who are behind him, and in whose generalship and experience he has the greatest confidence. Thus we are enabled to use men in large and important enterprises, who left to themselves would be comparatively powerless and unsuccessful. What can prevent our over-running the whole kingdom for our divine Master?

Of course, anyone may look down upon us in our present small development. They may very easily find out many grievous defects and weaknesses. We know, alas! of only too many ourselves, for we can look closely and critically at our affairs, as well as triumphantly at our God. Much of this book will probably be set down to the "enthusiasm of the writer." But, stay; "the enthusiasm of the writer" daily increases by intercourse with these crowds of poor believers no less enthusiastic, to say the least of it, than himself. And the world knows how much enthusiasm can do on any battlefield, before any fortress! It is God that has made enthusiasts of us, and by His power we shall do valiantly.

As soon as God will give us the means, we shall deliberately prepare many amongst our people who are longing to go into the work, for such an enterprise—and then !

Let us not be misunderstood. We shall never, we trust, so utterly mistake our path as to encourage any one to try to ape the ministry. We trust the Christian Mission will never be crippled with a college, a theological seminary, a mutual improvement society, or a singing class.

Our cathedral is the open air, our college is the prayer-room, our library the Bible, our sanctuary the theatre, our diplomas the blackguards turned into preachers at our services. We have only to drill suitable men and women to use daringly and persistently the sword of the Spirit in the way it has been used by the Mission all along, and then to send them off to conquer wherever they go, and this they will do as long as they put their whole trust in God.

See, we have got an organization managed upon the simple business-like principles of a railway, with all the cohesion and co-operative force of a trades' union, formed of people whose devotion, determination, and confidence at least equals that of the Jesuits, and yet all of whom are left to enjoy and to use that perfect spiritual freedom and independence which only the Holy Ghost can bestow upon any man. We have nothing to lose. We are sure that we are destined by the God we serve and trust, to win.

Hinder us, nobody can. They have despised us—they have slandered us ; above all, they have slandered the originator, the leader, the soul of the Mission. They have cheated and robbed and wronged and spoiled us. They have tried every device that can be imagined to injure us ; "but having obtained help of God we continue unto this day," and by His help we should continue to exalt His name amongst the perishing multitudes of our country, if every friend we had became our foe to-morrow.

BUT YOU OUGHT TO HELP US, IF YOU CAN. WILL YOU ?

YOU WILL BE WELCOME

This Evening at Eight o'clock, at

THE PEOPLE'S HALL,

Whitechapel Road, London, E.,
East Corner of Bethnal Green Road,
Havelock Road, Wells Street, Hackney,
High Street, Stoke Newington,
East End of Commercial Road, Limehouse,
Kerbey Street, Poplar,
Fox Street, Canning Town,
Upper Road, Plaistow,
Town Quay, Barking,
Redmore Road, Hammersmith,
Tamworth Road, Croydon,
The Brook, Chatham,
High Street, Hastings,
St. Leonard's.
Lake Road, Landport, Portsmouth,
Bute Road, Cardiff,
St. John Street, Wellingboro',
Foundry Lane, Belgrave Gate, Leicester,
Briggate, Leeds,
Infirmary Street, Bradford,
Old Town Hall, Whitby,
Linthorpe Mews, Middlesbro',
Nelson Street, Middlesboro,
Market Square, North Ormesby,
The Old Theatre, Stockton-on-Tees,
The Salvation Theatre, East Hartlepool,
The Temperance Hall, West Hartlepool.

OR AT

Any Building used by us the day you read this.

[P. T. O.

YOU WILL BE WELCOME

NEXT SUNDAY,

At 7 or 11 a.m., 3 or 7 p.m., or other service hour,

At any of the Halls named on the other side,

OR AT

The Town Hall, Hammersmith,

The Lecture Hall, High Street, Chatham,

The Market Hall, Hastings,

The Stuart Hall, Cardiff,

The Salvation Warehouse, Leicester,

Pullan's Theatre, Bradford,

The Oddfellows' Hall, Middlesboro',

The Prince of Wales' Music Hall, Middlesboro',

The Star Theatre, Stockton-on-Tees,

The Salvation Theatre, East Hartlepool,

The Theatre Royal, West Hartlepool,

The St. Hilda's Music Hall, Whitby,

OR AT

Any Building used by the Christian Mission on that date.

———

Any saint is welcome to speak in any experience meeting, or to pray in any prayer meeting for three minutes.

For EU product safety concerns, contact us at Calle de José Abascal, 56–1°,
28003 Madrid, Spain or eugpsr@cambridge.org.

 www.ingramcontent.com/pod-product-compliance
Ingram Content Group UK Ltd.
Pitfield, Milton Keynes, MK11 3LW, UK
UKHW012343130625
459647UK00009B/501